NO BOUNDARIES
BREAK THROUGH TO SUPPLY CHAIN EXCELLENCE

JAMES A. TOMPKINS, PH.D.

TOMPKINS

Library of Congress Control Number 2003100515

Tompkins, James A.
        No boundaries : break through to supply chain
    excellence / James A. Tompkins.
            p. cm.
            Includes bibliographical references and index.
            ISBN 1-930426-04-6

        1. Business logistics.   I. Title.

HD38.5T663 2003   658.5
                                QBI03-200048
    Printed in Canada

Contents

Acknowledgements

Twenty-one months ago when I wrote the acknowledgements to the first edition, *No Boundaries: Moving Beyond Supply Chain Management*, I called the book an "exciting endeavor." Now, due to the unbelievable growth of our business and pace of supply chain innovation, I think I should call this edition a "wild journey." Along with me on this journey have been our 200 employees and more than 100 clients.

Allow me to thank the leaders of Tompkins Associates for their awesome work that allowed me the time to write this book:

Mark Buffum	Tony Gerace	John Seidl
Tiffany Burns	Dale Harmelink	Jerry Smith
Mike Futch	Denny McKnight	John Spain

Also of special note is the editorial staff of Tompkins Press and the marketing communications staff of Tompkins Associates. Of particular note here are Kami Spangenberg and Ron Gallagher, without whom this book would have been birthed.

Additionally, the support, love, and patience of my family has been key to allowing me to finish this work.

Lastly, I wish to thank a large number of global clients who have allowed us to help them enhance their Supply Chain Excellence capabilities and, thus, move beyond the hype of the supply chain and achieve true supply chain results.

James A. Tompkins, Ph.D.
January 1, 2003
Tompkins Associates, Inc.
Raleigh, North Carolina
jtompkins@tompkinsinc.com

Preface

Welcome to *No Boundaries*—or perhaps welcome back.

Those of you who read the first edition will find that I have significantly expanded the body of knowledge of the supply chain. For those of you who are joining the journey for the first time, welcome aboard. The journey to Supply Chain Excellence is about to begin!

Following my own advice, I've gone beyond the boundary I had reached when I wrote the previous version of this book. The 2000 edition introduced the concept of supply chain synthesis, the melting and blurring of the borders that have distinguished supply chain links and kept supply chains from achieving all they could, from winning against their competition. In this edition, I explain how supply chain synthesis is, in fact, one point on a spectrum of steps in the journey to Supply Chain Excellence.

Synthesis is a very, very important step—the fifth out of six, critical to achieve, and the result only of much hard work. Now, however, I can lay out for you the continuum through which companies move in pursuit of Supply Chain Excellence. We understand more as leaders than we knew two years ago, but the title of the book is still much the same because the basic message remains valid: boundaries break supply chains and kill businesses, and the only way to excel in the future is to tear down boundaries and build partnerships, to forge borderless supply chains that unite all their partners in an uncompromising focus on satisfying the end-user.

I didn't know I had reached a boundary last time; sometimes boundaries are visible only in hindsight. That just proves that no company and no leader can stand pat. Businesses and business leaders must continuously improve.

Welcome to the path forward.

Introduction

This is not your parents' economy. The vertical behemoths of the 20th century that supported mass production and focused only on themselves are disappearing and are being replaced with lean, deverticalized, virtual, and global organizations. Now, companies that were established in the old economy must redirect their focus from internal to external in order to succeed. They can no longer let company versus company drive their business plans, but instead must think in terms of supply chain versus supply chain.

Tompkins clients are no different. They've been reading, doing the math, and reorganizing. Initial meetings with these clients often focus on Supply Chain Excellence. Some have tried to achieve it, yet it remains out of their reach. Others want to achieve it but do not know where to start. Where they are now seems so far from Supply Chain Excellence that they are overwhelmed.

As I study their attempts, problems, and failures, the same thing becomes apparent: These clients are either trying to do too much too fast or trying to cut corners. Yes, speed is key, but even people who run fast still have to get from point A to point Z by traveling past points B, C, D and so on. Achieving Supply Chain Excellence is like climbing a ladder: If you start at the bottom and try to get to the top by skipping rungs, the end result will most likely be a fall, complete with injuries.

Another thing I've realized is that Supply Chain Management (SCM) has not produced the desired results, mainly because many companies think that SCM is the secret to Supply Chain Excellence. Actually, SCM is important to Supply Chain Excellence because it creates Link Excellence, Level 2 on the path to Supply Chain Excellence, but it is only one rung on the ladder and not the ultimate destination. Other companies have given up on SCM to chase the supply chain fads of Efficient Consumer Response (ECR), Quick Response (QR), and Just-in-Time (JIT) manufacturing and distribution and have experienced disappointing results. In fact, according to a report on the state of logistics in 2002, in the food sector, there has been little to no decrease in raw materials, WIP, or finished good inventory between 1981 and 2002. That's 21 years of stagnant inventory!

To compound problems, supply chain software is typically used inside an organization, rather than across the links of the supply chain. The right software can achieve results within the organization, but it brings no value to the total supply chain if it stops there. The customer continues to be dissatisfied. Why? Because information must be shared throughout the supply chain's communications network, not just by departments of individual links. If information is not shared and accessible to all links of the supply chain, the customer's needs and desires are lost somewhere in the information silos.

The results of information silos are slow information, distorted information, and no information. One industry knows all too well the role poor information plays in creating an inefficient supply chain. The Automotive Industry Action Group (AIAG) says that "just in case" inventories associated with information disconnects cost the industry $1 billion annually. Every automobile produced in the United States could cost, on average, $70 less with a better supply chain strategy.

Some believed that the "Information Superhighway" would change all that. In recent years, however, we've read and heard a lot about the dot-com to dot-bomb phenomenon. According to Boston Consulting Group, from September 1999 to October 2000, more than 100 dot-coms failed. Some went bankrupt, others made huge cuts in their work force, and others drastically rewrote their business plans. Most of them simply shut down their Web sites.

As the dust settles, it seems everyone has a theory about what went wrong. Most experts, however, blame the failures on several things:

1. Emphasis on revenues, not profits
2. Poor business models
3. Interest rate hikes in 2000
4. Zero inventory
5. IPO euphoria
6. Unwise investment

They go on to assume that e- is dead. Companies that had grandiose plans of creating B2B cyber marketplaces, extranets, and trading portals have either scaled back their plans or put them on hold indefinitely. The attitude is, "Well, we tried e-, but it didn't work. Now, it's back to the old ways of doing business."

My answer to that is simple. All assumptions are wrong. These doomsday prophets are looking down a mineshaft, unable to see the peak of the mountain above them, let alone the peak of the next mountain to climb. The Internet is still the most important invention of the last 100 years. It has irrevocably changed the way we do business, the way our customers shop, the way we manufacture products. It has and will continue to totally reinvent business in ways we can only imagine.

The reality is that the dot-com to dot-bomb phenomenon was about laying the groundwork for what the Internet and World Wide Web will be. Now we can get past the euphoria and the hype and use the Internet and Web as they really should be used: as communications tools that allow all supply chain partners to work at the same time rather than sequentially and to respond nimbly and agilely to events and overwhelming change like the events of September 11, 2001.

It is also time for companies to understand the process of achieving Supply Chain Excellence and where SCM fits in Supply Chain Excellence. SCM can help your company achieve Link Excellence, but it is Supply Chain Excellence that will bring you and your supply chain increased return on assets (ROA), improved customer satisfaction, maximized speed, reduced costs, and the integration of the total supply chain. It will assure that your Internet and Web communications translate to real results and that your chain will achieve a competitive advantage over all competing chains.

This book will introduce you to the Six Levels of Supply Chain Excellence and the eight core competencies necessary for moving up the levels. It will also show you how you can achieve awesome supply chain results with technology. The supply chains you create with this book will be agile and will have No Boundaries, and the result will be tremendous competitive advantage. Achieving Supply Chain Excellence is a bold new journey, but it is the only way to travel. For those who want to win in today's global marketplace, it's time to begin the journey.

1

Beyond Supply Chain Management

"When there are no limits to whom you see, where you'll go, what you'll touch, the results are remarkable."

— Jack Welch, former CEO, GE

Industry is looking for an answer. What is the question? Simply, it is "How do we keep our customers happy, grow our business, and increase profitability?"

The answer to this question used to be "Supply Chain Management." For 15 years, Supply Chain Management (SCM) has tried to be the panacea for poor customer service, poor communication, and poor relationships. Yet, despite all of our SCM efforts, we are still losing ground. According to a Spring 2002 article in *Supply Chain Management Review,* "Companies are investing in software, hiring consultants, and reconfiguring their physical supply chains in order to capture the promised returns from lean supply chain management. Yet the returns from these investments can be elusive."

This is not due to neglect of the supply chain. Instead, the reason that SCM has not yielded the desired results is because it has been treated as the *only* and *ultimate* way to make customers happy, grow business, and increase profitability when, in reality, it is part of a much bigger solution: Supply Chain Excellence. SCM is about optimizing individual links, and this is very important in the process of linking to a supply chain. However, it is not sufficient. Competition today is not about my link versus your link; competition today is my chain versus your chain.

To deliver maximum value, customization, and satisfaction to the ultimate customer while reducing inventory, trimming lead times, and reducing costs, the supply chain must become one agile entity, with No Boundaries, the goal of which is to satisfy the ultimate customer. To do this, the supply chain must advance through six distinct levels. These levels are:

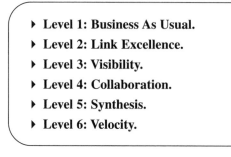

> ▸ **Level 1: Business As Usual.**
> ▸ **Level 2: Link Excellence.**
> ▸ **Level 3: Visibility.**
> ▸ **Level 4: Collaboration.**
> ▸ **Level 5: Synthesis.**
> ▸ **Level 6: Velocity.**

These six levels are addressed more fully in Chapter 3.

Achieving Supply Chain Excellence is a process. It's not important where an organization is in the process, as long as it moves up step-by-step. Think of a ladder: If you start at the bottom rung and try to get to the top by skipping rungs, the end result will most likely be a fall, complete with injuries. If you move step by step, however, you will reach accelerated synthesis, or Supply Chain Excellence.

What is Supply Chain Excellence?

Supply Chain Excellence is the ultimate supply chain process. It is a holistic, continuous improvement process of ensuring customer satisfaction from the original raw material provider to the ultimate, finished-product consumer. In other words, it is doing business with No Boundaries. It is holistic because it is concerned with a complete chain, rather than one link. It is a continuous improvement process that is infinite; it never stops. When a supply chain achieves Supply Chain Excellence, its links run together into a smooth, agile, continuous flow. Visualize a river, properly banked and channeled, that is flowing toward a goal and you are also visualizing Supply Chain Excellence. A river has no links, and although thousands of separate, natural forces comprise it, it is seen as one entity.

From Chain to River

"Without banks the river is just a puddle."

— Mark Twain

A river must have banks, or as Mark Twain says, it will be a puddle. The Supply Chain Excellence riverbanks are integration and change. Without one or the other or both,

Supply Chain Excellence is nothing but a puddle, with no force or direction. The breadth of integration and the rate of change are creating movement and force, yet there seems to be a lack of understanding of the effect each has on the supply chain. If you gain a solid understanding of integration and change, it will provide you with a set of requirements for tomorrow's business climate.

In the 1980s, integrating within processes was the integration focus. Then, in the 1990s, the opportunity to integrate between processes became apparent, and SCM was born of this new focus. The thrust was to integrate manufacturing and distribution to create an integrated supply chain via SCM. SCM was viewed as the ultimate integration, and many companies and business gurus still believe this. It is easy to understand why: integration may be viewed at different levels, depending on the vantage point. If you are hovering six feet above the ground in a hot air balloon, then the worker in the workstation looks like integration. As your balloon goes up, you see integration as man/workstation/equipment, then as material handling systems, then as manufacturing systems, and then as SCM. You are now a mile above the ground, and your balloonist may tell you there is no need to go any higher or that there are greater risks at higher altitudes. But if you insist and he complies, then you reach the vantage point where integration is at its highest level: Supply Chain Excellence.

So, from an integration perspective, we see that there is a progressively expanding concept of what Supply Chain Excellence means and how it functions. A company's leadership must ride that balloon as high as it can go to have the broadest perspective and ensure its success. Part of that larger view includes the second riverbank—change.

There are two primary drivers of change. They are people and technology. Take some time to think about these facts:

1. In 1860, one billion people populated the planet. In 2002, that number reached 6.2 billion.
2. Eighty percent of technological advances have occurred since 1900.
3. Available information doubles every five years.

People are driving change because there are so many of us now. We went from one billion people in 1860, to two billion in 1935, to four billion in 1975, to six billion in 1999. Not only is the world growing, but it also is growing at an increasingly rapid rate. If you were to graph the "people" variables (length of life, income, transport speed, population) in the history of change, there would be a flat line, then a slight curve, and then a sharp curve. Today we are living in the sharp curve.

Say That Again?

There are a few quotes I want to share with you as we think about change:

▸ In 1876, Western Union, after an in-depth study, said, "The telephone has too many shortcomings to be seriously considered as a means of communication."
▸ Harry Warner, one of the Warner Brothers, said, "Who the hell wants to hear actors talk?"
▸ Early in the computer era, Ken Olson, the founder, president, and CEO of Digital Equipment Corp. and also the man who created one of the most successful computer companies in the country said, "There is no reason for any individual to have a computer in the home."
▸ Before September 11, 2001, when the question of national defense was raised, U.S. leaders discussed protecting ourselves from attacks carried out with traditional weapons of mass destruction.

Isn't it interesting to see what happens when we don't keep change in view? As business leaders, we must, with obsession, remember that we are in the sharp curve, lest we make an ill-informed decision about our industry and miss the boat.

Our ever-expanding population is living longer and becoming more demanding. In the days before automobiles, if a family that wanted to take a trip on a stagecoach was told, "Sorry, the stagecoach has already left. You've got to wait a week," they'd say, "No problem. It's only a week." Now, if we miss a section in a revolving door, we get upset. If we are caught by a red light, we start banging on the steering wheel and yelling, "I've got to go!"

Few people slow to the speed limit anymore. The time it takes for us to log onto our e-mail server seems to be forever, and we complain about how slow it is, when, in reality, it only takes about eight seconds.

In the U.S., another change being driven by people is where we work. In 1900, 85 percent of the population worked in agriculture, 10 percent in production, and 5 percent in service. Today, about 1 percent of the U.S. population works on the farm, 13 percent works in production, and 86 percent works in service. Yet, we are producing more wealth in agriculture—$200 billion in annual sales today—than we have ever produced in the history of our country. In manufacturing, we produce 23 percent of our gross domestic product in the factory. We are as strong in manufacturing as we have been any time since the statistics were first kept

in 1947. We have an agricultural-manu-
facturing based economy, not a service
economy. Sure, more people work in the
service sector, and productivity and yield
in agriculture and manufacturing have
grown to the point of not needing a lot
of people, but of the 86 percent of the
population that is in the service sector,
many people service the agricultural
and manufacturing sectors. The world's
economy is no longer driven by
resources; it is driven by knowledge.

Like the population, technology is
driving change because it is exploding.
The most dramatic explosion in technology is the Internet. Business transactions
on the Internet are increasing exponen-
tially. Consumer online sales hit $47.6
billion in 2001, a 12 percent increase
over 2000. On the business-to-business
(B2B) side, the average amount of
materials that companies bought online
jumped from 7.1 percent of all purchases
in the third quarter of 2001 to 9.5 percent in the fourth quarter.

With all these changes swirling
around us, it is difficult to predict the
future. I read a Putman Investments ad that said, "You think you understand the situation,
but what you don't understand is that the situation just changed." As soon as you know
something, everything changes. All assumptions are wrong. In 1900, it was predicted that
by 1919, everyone in America would be working in the fields and there would be a land
shortage. These seers missed the point on two issues: productivity and yield. As productivity and yield have grown, not only is there enough food for everyone to eat, but there
is enough to export. By the 1950s, many agricultural workers had left the farm and
gone to the factory. The seers predicted that by 1970, everyone would be in the factory

The Sharp Curve of Technology

As Lew Pritchett, formerly of Procter & Gamble, stated: "Success in the next century [21st] will depend on access to information, not access to capital." But how we shift culturally toward information attainment and utilization is a major issue. This may be most prevalent in the following observations:

▸ Web-based training is embraced by many companies even though half of the respondents in a recent EDS survey said they like traditional classroom training better.

▸ The worldwide smart card industry could reach $2.2 billion in revenue within the next few years—if the industry agrees on standards and depth of marketing efforts.

▸ XML may eliminate EDI—if industry agrees on standards and protocols for the data-driven mark-up language.

producing goods. They believed that, as the standard of living improved, people would try to acquire more things, thereby creating a need for more workers to produce them. The seers had learned nothing from the agriculture revolution and, once again, did not take change into account. Now, as we start a new century, we see that the number of people required to produce all those things they were imagining in the 1950s is 13 percent of the population.

Seers who believed they had a handle on the Internet revolution missed the boat when addressing the impact it is having on business. These pundits discounted people in their prophecy. The Internet, because it connects people and information quicker, easier, and at minimal cost, allows people to make better decisions. Buyers can easily compare products, prices, and services, as well as communicate with far more people than they have in the past. New relationships are forged daily, and, when they are vendor-customer relationships, the playing field is leveled, reducing the value of branding and accelerating margin pressures. The importance of providing quality service and high levels of customer satisfaction becomes paramount.

Like all seers past and present, if you attempt to look at anything without understanding the impact of change, you will fall on your face. Your business will not work. Yet, many are doing exactly that with SCM. They think they are improving the supply chain with SCM because they don't realize that SCM focuses only on the optimization of a static environment. The only way to handle change and the dynamic environment that is the result of change is by using an agile, continuous improvement process that addresses changing requirements as they occur.

Management by Fad

Many people think that approaches are the way to harness change. It is much easier to grasp an approach than it is to understand and implement a process. An approach focus, rather than a process focus, creates what I call Management by Fad (MBF). When what they are doing isn't working, people often reach out and grab first one thing and then another. First they do it, then they re-do it, then they are beyond re-doing it. They engineer, reengineer, re-reengineer, and then they are beyond engineering. They try on a new technique and keep insisting it fits until the seams finally burst. They then go in search of the next style and size. Many wait for an expert to arrive and explain the next technique so that they may print a slogan on a coffee mug and feel better.

Today's challenges cannot be resolved by shellacking a layer of fad over them. We must ride that balloon to the highest level and look at the panorama that it creates, using our framework of integration and change. Supply Chain Excellence and agility will power us to that level and let us see not just today's challenges, but challenges that we can't even imagine at this point.

Where Do We Go from Here?

The vision of the future requires us to move beyond the SCM approach. Before that happens, however, we must take a hard look at SCM to see how the approach can be used as a building block for a process—the process of achieving Supply Chain Excellence. SCM is truly a logistical concept. It is not something you view from a total supply chain point of view. Supply Chain Excellence is a total supply chain point of view and to do it well, we must do not only logistics, but also manufacturing, maintenance, quality, and organizational excellence. That is why SCM has a place in the Six Levels of Supply Chain Excellence, but it is not Supply Chain Excellence and never will be.

This book presents, in detail, how SCM works in the context of the Six Levels of Supply Chain Excellence, how Supply Chain Excellence can enable your organization to reach unparalleled levels of performance, how any organization can use the eight core competencies required to create an agile supply chain, and the technology that can assist in that process.

2

What's Going on Today?

"All change is a miracle to contemplate; but it is a miracle which is taking place every second."

— Henry David Thoreau

So much is happening. The sharp curve we discussed in Chapter 1 is changing the way we view business. We are also being presented with various challenges. SKUs continue to grow, boundaries between manufacturing and distribution are blurring, deverticalization—a de-layering activity that creates the opposite of a vertical industry—is becoming a trend, and security and nimbleness in business have become more important in the wake of September 11, 2001. These have also brought about what I consider the major challenges of change: channel structure and relationships, customer satisfaction, information systems and technology, a global economy, virtual factories, and the evolution from a nimble to an agile enterprise. All of these challenges must be viewed through the filters of integration and change.

Channel Structure and Relationships

In today's business climate, channel structures are blurring and relationships are fluid. Industry is removing links from the supply chain through de-layering, outsourcing, deverticalization, and the virtual factory, and alternate channels such as catalogs and the Internet are growing tremendously. Not only will that growth rate continue, but it will also increase, particularly for outsourcing. For example, the last decade saw a surge in growth of contract electronic manufacturers (CEMs) and third-party logistics providers (3PLs). Today's CEMs are offering more manufacturing, design, and logistics services to original equipment manufacturers (OEMs) than ever before. According to *Purchasing* magazine, the people who handle purchasing for OEMs say their companies save about 25 percent

The Value of Outsourcing – Solectron

Solectron, one of the largest contract manufacturers in the world, was cited as the No. 3 organization in the 1999 Business Week Info Tech 100 and was ranked 110th in the Fortune 500 list in 2002. Its global presence includes representation in 21 countries. Solectron's dominance in the CEM market can be traced to several factors:

- Its efficiency
- Its ability to exploit its high volume
- Its willingness to provide value-added services to original equipment manufacturers like Nortel, Lucent, Microsoft, Juniper Networks, and Cisco.

As for efficiency, Solectron spends almost nothing on frills, and its overhead is 4 percent of sales. By virtue of its diverse and large customer base, the company can leverage itself against vendors to receive discounts on materials, and Solectron passes these discounts on to the OEM. Solectron also derives more use out of each piece of equipment as a result of its order volume. Finally, this CEM takes on the less glamorous aspects of manufacturing and repair, as well as logistics and purchasing, enabling its OEMs to concentrate on high-level design and brand recognition.

of manufacturing costs by outsourcing production to CEMs. Logistics outsourcing has also seen a marked increase. A survey conducted in 2001 reveals that 74 percent of the America's largest manufacturing companies use 3PLs, more than double the percentage a decade earlier. Also, 60 percent of those surveyed rely on 3PLs for warehouse management, and nearly 40 percent outsource part of their order-fulfillment services. Even more telling is the fact that these manufacturers expect to increase the amount of money spent on 3PL outsourcing from 25 percent to 34 percent by 2004.

Information technology (IT) is also developing outsourcing relationships. A proliferation of application service providers (ASPs), third-party entities that manage and distribute software-based services and solutions to customers across a wide area network from a central data center, has emerged as a result of Y2K fears. These ASPs allow companies to outsource some or all of their IT needs. A number of technology analysts predict that the total ASP market will increase from $3 billion in 2001 to roughly $16.1 billion by 2005.

The impact that outsourcing, de-layering, deverticalization, and virtual factories have on channel structures and relationships is mind-boggling. Sometimes they add links to the supply chain, and sometimes they remove links. Whether they add or subtract links, they have major effects on how businesses are organized and they require partnerships along the supply chain that leap over one of the highest hurdles in American business: the "us versus them" mentality of supplier/customer relationships.

Recent trends in commerce, such as supplier certification, provide added value to the end product and strengthen the supply chain as a result. Ultimately, those who truly understand and practice partnerships will triumph as the structures of channels and relationships change.

Customer Satisfaction

Customization, customer choice, customer control, customer relationship management, and customer-centric thinking are increasingly being used to describe business focus, a change from the enterprise-wide focus that characterized it just a few years ago. As Janet Gould, in her article in the June 1999 issue of IDS, wrote, "The 'good old days'—when Henry Ford dictated that the customer could have his Model T in any color as long as it was black—are history." Basically, customer needs and desires are dictating what manufacturers produce—and any business that does not listen will be left behind.

The Value of Partnering in the Japanese Auto Industry

At one time, Japanese automakers were firmly against partnerships with carmakers from other countries. However, this attitude has changed for two of Japan's automakers, Mitsubishi and Nissan. In the last three years, both have used partnerships to end a downward slump in sales and profits.

Under a partnership with DaimlerChrysler that was formed in 2000, Mitsubishi cut about 6,400 jobs in the third quarter of 2001, about 10 percent of its global work force. The company, under the guidance of DaimlerChrysler AG executive Rolf Eckrodt, became profitable after two consecutive years of losses. The alliance is expected to help cut costs on development and purchasing, and the two automakers are working on a new small car together.

After Nissan entered a partnership with Renault SA of France in 1999, Carlos Ghosn, the French-educated Brazilian executive who left Renault to became Nissan president, began cutting costs and reducing debt. In the first quarter of 2002, Nissan returned to profitability and has begun launching new vehicles, including a crossover SUV and a new sports coupe under its Infiniti brand.

And because customers are now dictating what is being produced, customer satisfaction has become paramount.

Part of the challenge of customer satisfaction for many companies is understanding that it is not the same as traditional customer service. The basic formula for customer satisfaction is:

Customer Satisfaction = Customer Perception of the Service Received –
Customer Expectation of Customer Service.

The customer satisfaction formula presupposes three critical statements that every organization seeking to revolutionize customer satisfaction must assimilate:

1. Customer satisfaction is based on our customers' perceptions and expectations, not on our self-centered view of what the customer may want.
2. The level of customer satisfaction will change as customers' expectations change— and they can change almost daily.
3. We must anticipate customers' expectations and needs based on their habits and patterns.

Customer satisfaction requires us to divest our self-interest and to focus on the needs, expectations, and perceptions of those to whom we provide products and services. Because customers change while they are our customers, companies cannot maintain customer satisfaction with the same set of services and value-adds that satisfied the customer yesterday. As customers progress in their patronage, they require more to be satisfied. For our customer satisfaction to be high, we must separate our customers into categories or tiers. These tiers—visitors, associates, and partners—should then be treated in a way that reflects the profit they bring us.

This separation helps us enjoy customers that are highly satisfied while maximizing our profit. With so many new demands, like the SKU explosion and increased product cus-tomization, being placed on companies every day, the ability to keep customer satisfaction levels high will be critical. This will especially be true as these two trends continue their rapid growth in the years to come.

How will you be able to keep up while significantly improving customer satisfaction? Supply Chain Excellence can answer that question. By removing the boundaries between all the links in the chain and creating an agile river, you will be able to know your customers, serve your customers, and satisfy your customers. You will develop new practices that can anticipate individual customer needs and expectations and meet them with products and services that represent unique value for each customer. The flow of supply chain communications will allow demand planning, data mining to create a data chain, trimmed lead-times, cost reductions, and quality improvements. The creativity of the entire supply chain will be brought to bear on the ultimate customer's needs.

Information Systems and Technology

Many of us have a difficult time remembering the days before voice mail and e-mail, LANs, WANs, and VANs, intranets and extranets, video conferencing and whiteboarding, streaming and Webcasts. Information technology (IT) can make us crazy, but it is undoubtedly a driving force in bringing our world closer. Applied correctly, it brings out the best in our people and harnesses creativity in team and individual environments.

IT is moving forward faster than we can imagine. The Internet is connecting people and information quicker, easier, and at a minimal cost. The World Wide Web has evolved from a place for brochureware to a place for dialogue and relationships, a place to resolve differences between systems and platforms, and a tool for learning more about individual customers. This levels the playing field among competitors and accelerates margin pressures, makes it harder to establish a brand, and increases the importance of providing quality service.

Off the Web, Auto ID, communications technology, and business software are being standardized, and systems integrators are writing custom interfaces to allow the exchange of data among applications. Also, middleware is developing rapidly, creating ways to tie disparate programs and systems together through enterprise application integrators (EAIs) and Web application servers.

With IT, companies can extend their market reach and accomplish things beyond the scope of current imagination. IT is the key to Visibility, Level 3 of Supply Chain Excellence, and Collaboration, Level 4. At a Supply Chain Collaboration and Visibility Roundtable conducted in August 2001, the participants reached the following conclusion: "Supply chain visibility and collaboration capabilities are evolving rapidly . . . ." Added Frank Cicio, former Senior Vice President and General Manager, Tradestream at Optum, a technology company that develops cross-enterprise solutions, "We're at the very early stages of a new frontier." Imagine the possibilities once the frontier becomes an established settlement!

Global Economy

The success of firms depends heavily now on their ability to reach foreign markets. Business no longer ends at the border of a particular country or the edge of a continent. "No Boundaries" is more than a phrase. Two factors have affected this new global economy: politics and technology. Politically, the last two decades have eliminated some of the isolationism that has plagued business. Trade agreements have been established to ease the tensions and reticence between once-competing nations. Major trade agreements made in the last two decades include:

- North American Free Trade Agreement (NAFTA)—between Canada, the United States, and Mexico
- Southern Common Market (Mercosur)—between Argentina, Brazil, Paraguay, and Uruguay
- Andean Pact—between Bolivia, Colombia, Ecuador, Peru, and Venezuela
- Central American Common Market—between Costa Rica, El Salvador, Guatemala, Honduras, and Nicaragua
- European Union (EU)—formation of a single economic market in Europe integrated further by the introduction of the Euro, a currency shared by most of its members.

Technology also plays a role in this global economy. The Internet has made the world smaller, and, in fact, has made geography irrelevant. With the speed of information delivery and the shrinking distances that it creates between markets, the supply chains we are competing against may be halfway around the world rather than across town. In many cases, when we are using the Internet to disseminate information, we may not even know where the person or company is to whom we are sending it.

New trade agreements, individual countries partnering with each other to produce and export goods, international e-commerce, and Web applications are only a few of the many challenges presented by the global marketplace. Their numbers will continue to increase. To address them robustly, we must be agile and we must achieve Supply Chain Excellence.

Virtual Factories

Focused factories, deverticalization, and the ease of sharing information all have a hand in creating the concept of virtual factories. An office furniture manufacturing company, for example, may not manufacture chairs in its plant. Instead, it may assemble chairs from parts that arrive from all over the world. Production and scheduling, along with shipping and supply ordering, are conducted in real-time or via the World Wide Web. Virtual factories, therefore, are really enterprises that gather, organize, select, synthesize, and distribute information and parts with information technology, be it Electronic Data Interchange (EDI), the Internet, or a combination of technology.

In these virtual entities, the concepts of economies of scale and scope of ability do not apply. Instead, virtual factory and enterprise processes are built on relationships with customers and strategic partners with an eye to anticipating and proactively handling inventory, production costs, product design, capacity planning, training, and other aspects of manufacturing differently. Various strategies are being developed and utilized so that manufacturing is still possible within these virtual environments. Lean manufacturing principles, in particular, are gaining momentum because they can transform huge, outdated manufacturing monoliths into sleek, lean, flexible, and agile operations.

The Myths of the Past

The unbelievable rate of change affects everything that takes place. At the time that we accept this concept, we must also put a myth behind us: In business, the past is a good indicator of the future. Nowhere is this more evident than in our fast-paced, merger-and-acquisition world. A client that, two months ago, was two completely different companies is at present one company with a combination of 44 distribution centers. If this company relies on its past to predict its future, it will go out of business.

We should not ignore the past. Instead, we should understand that the future is an extension of the present based upon the background of the past. The future is not an extension of the past, and if we are to meet today's challenges, create a vision for the future, and achieve Supply Chain Excellence, we must remember that.

3

The Six Levels of Supply Chain Excellence: A Foundation for the Future

"There will be two types of companies in the future. The quick and the dead."

— Charles B. Wang, Chairman Emeritus, Computer Associates International

People are always trying to forecast the future. Many base their forecasts on the past. This is a mistake that can catch us all. If we examine the word "forecast" carefully, we can see how forecasting is bound to fail. In the game of golf, the word "fore" can signal to passersby "duck!" When they go fishing, people "cast," which means "to throw out." If we are alternately ducking and throwing out, we are reacting and not predicting. In most cases, we are reacting to the past and using it as our foundation for predicting the future. It used to work, but because of the rate of change now, that foundation is crumbling. It is time to replace that inflexible foundation with a new, agile one: Supply Chain Excellence.

Supply Chain Excellence comprises six distinct levels, and the key to achieving these levels has two edges: harnessing the energy of change to become agile and integrating the total supply chain. Harnessing the energy of change to become agile is discussed in Chapter 7. The results of integrating the total supply chain form the adhesive for Supply Chain Excellence. This chapter discusses the Six Levels of Supply Chain Excellence in detail and the characteristics of integrating the total supply chain in that context.

The Six Levels of Supply Chain Excellence

Attaining Supply Chain Excellence is a process. It has six steps, or levels. It is not important where an organization is in the process, as long as it is moving up step-by-step. The levels are Business as Usual, Link Excellence, Visibility, Collaboration, Synthesis, and Velocity. The sections that follow describe these steps.

Business as Usual

Business as Usual is when a company is working hard to maximize its individual functions. The finance, marketing, sales, purchasing, information technology, research and development, manufacturing, distribution, and human resources departments are each trying to be the best in the company. Organizational effectiveness is not the emphasis. Each organizational element only attempts to function well within its silo.

Link Excellence

Today's organizations usually have numerous departments and facilities, including plants, warehouses, and distribution centers (DCs). If an organization hopes to pursue Supply Chain Excellence, it must look at the entire company, eliminate any boundaries between departments and facilities, and begin a never-ending journey of continuous improvement.

In actuality, no organization should even begin to think about achieving Supply Chain Excellence until it has evolved itself into the most efficient, effective, responsive, and holistic link that it can possibly be. This requires mastering demand management, which means studying patterns of customer demand and using them to meet customer needs and expectations. An example is a supermarket chain that may not realize that when it puts wine on sale, it might want to consider two other things: putting cheese on sale and moving the cheese department so that it is adjacent to the wine department. Market research has shown that those who buy wine are also likely to purchase cheese. If the supermarket's link isn't whole, it may not know this information, thereby losing an opportunity to capitalize on cheese sales.

An organization pursuing Supply Chain Excellence must have strategic and tactical initiatives at the department, plant, and link levels for design and systems. Also critical are systems and software at the department, plant, and link levels that create organizational readiness for Supply Chain Excellence. If an organization is not ready for Supply Chain Excellence, it will not be able to achieve it. This fact is unavoidable and non-negotiable.

At this point, some of the initiatives can use logistics and SCM, as long as the organization remembers that neither will take it beyond Link Excellence. Therefore, Link Excellence is where SCM should be positioned in the process of achieving Supply Chain Excellence.

Visibility

Supply Chain Excellence requires everyone along the supply chain to work together. However, partners in the supply chain cannot work together if they cannot see one another. Visibility, the third level of Supply Chain Excellence, brings to light all links in the supply chain. "Implementing visibility in the supply chain has actually turned the lights on to the whole process. The thing that is really compelling is that visibility reveals the areas that aren't working—that is the real impact it has had. And that, in turn, brings about collaboration," says Jon Kirkegaard, Executive Vice President, Chief Marketing Officer, Vizional Technologies, Inc.

Visibility also minimizes supply chain surprises because it provides the information that links need to understand the ongoing order status. It could be considered the first "real" step away from the organization and toward Supply Chain Excellence. Through Visibility, organizations come to understand their roles in a supply chain and are aware of the other links. An example is an electronics distributor with a Web site that allows its customers to input circuit board designs and then funnels information about those circuit boards to suppliers. Visibility thus requires sharing information so that the links understand the ongoing order status and demand planning becomes possible.

Sharing information requires trust and technology. Both are critical if a supply chain wishes to achieve Visibility. Without trust, organizations cannot achieve Visibility or move to the fourth level of Supply Chain Excellence. Without technology, Visibility is not possible. Furthermore, Visibility requires more than vanilla-flavored software. You must know your company's needs and your supply chain's needs to select the correct Visibility technology. A business application that is suitable for Ford may not work for IBM. If someone has a wooden ladder, a metal rung will not fit it. Therefore, it is important to develop a strategic plan to acquire the right application for your supply chain's true needs.

Collaboration

Once a supply chain achieves Visibility, it can move to Collaboration, the fourth level of Supply Chain Excellence. Through Collaboration, the supply chain can determine how best to meet the demands of the marketplace. The supply chain works as a whole to maximize customer satisfaction while minimizing inventories.

Collaboration is achieved through the proper application of technology and true partnerships. Various Collaboration technologies exist, and, as with Visibility software, the supply chain must choose the right technology or combination of technologies if it hopes

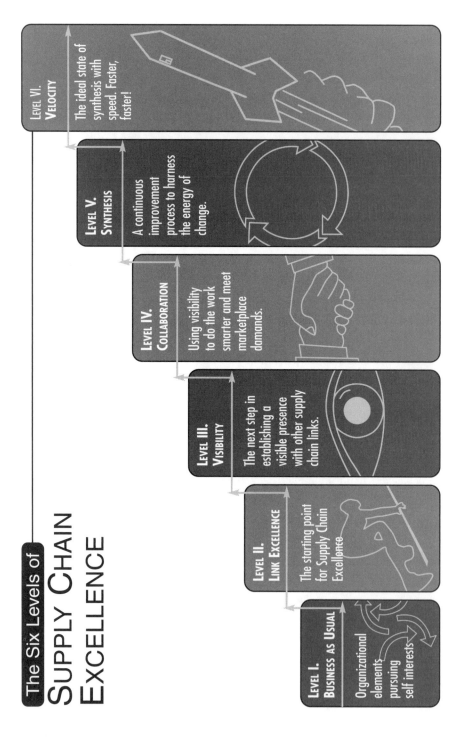

The Six Levels of
SUPPLY CHAIN
EXCELLENCE

LEVEL VI.
VELOCITY

The ideal state of synthesis with speed. Faster, faster!

LEVEL V.
SYNTHESIS

A continuous improvement process to harness the energy of change.

LEVEL IV.
COLLABORATION

Using visibility to do the work smarter and meet marketplace demands.

LEVEL III.
VISIBILITY

The next step in establishing a visible presence with other supply chain links.

LEVEL II.
LINK EXCELLENCE

The starting point for Supply Chain Excellence

LEVEL I.
BUSINESS AS USUAL

Organizational elements pursuing self interests

to collaborate properly. True partnerships require total commitment from all the links in the supply chain and are based on trust and a mutual desire to work as one for the benefit of the supply chain.

Synthesis

Once Collaboration is achieved, the supply chain then pursues the continuous improvement process of Synthesis so that it can harness the energy of change and become agile. Synthesis is the synchronization of all supply chain links to form a whole. It creates a complete pipeline with a customer perspective that allows the supply chain to anticipate customer needs rather than react to them. Synthesis differs from Collaboration because of this anticipation. Collaboration creates a nimble supply chain that waits for a problem to occur before solving it, but Synthesis creates an agile one through supply chain planning that expects and solves the problem before it happens. This is accomplished with the proper demand planning technology and skills.

The results of Synthesis are:

- *Increased return on assets (ROA)*—achieved by maximizing inventory turns, minimizing obsolete inventory, maximizing employee participation, and maximizing continuous improvement.
- *Improved customer satisfaction*—achieved because Synthesis creates companies that are responsive to the customer's needs through customization. They understand value-added activity. They also understand flexibility and how to meet ever-changing customer requirements. They completely comprehend the meaning of high quality and strive to provide high value.
- *Reduced costs*—achieved by scrutinizing transportation costs, acquisition costs, distribution costs, inventory carrying costs, reverse logistics costs, packaging costs, and others and by continually searching for ways to drive costs down.
- *An integrated supply chain*—achieved by using partnerships and communication to integrate the supply chain and focus on the ultimate customer.

In summary, supply chains that reach the Synthesis level are going to have major successes. A few already have; they include Dell and Wal-Mart. They accomplished this with patience and demand planning. Synthesis is not achieved overnight. It takes time to take the links of a supply chain and remove the boundaries between them. However, if all links are visible and all collaborate, then Synthesis is within reach.

Velocity

Today's business environment demands speed. The Internet has created immediate orders, and customer expectations that their products will arrive almost as quickly. Velocity is Synthesis at the speed of light. It creates multi-level networks that meet these demands—complex entities that can meet the demands of today's economy through a combination of partnerships, flexibility, robust design methods, demand planning, and agility. The emphasis changes from designing systems and networks that work to designing systems and networks that work and work fast. It is the process that will achieve not only Supply Chain Excellence, but ongoing Supply Chain Excellence.

Supply chains that pursue the journey to Supply Chain Excellence are going to have major successes today and in the future. To make Supply Chain Excellence happen, it is important to be armed with knowledge and the spirit of collaboration and cooperation. Along with integration of the total supply chain, this spirit will enable your organization and your supply chain to reach unparalleled levels of performance, synthesize the supply chain, and apply the technology that can assist in that process.

Integration of the Total Supply Chain: The Tie That Binds

A recurring theme runs throughout each of the Six Levels of Supply Chain Excellence, and that has one recurring theme that runs throughout, and that theme is integration. If your systems are not integrated at each level, you will not be able to get to the next one. Your entire supply chain must be integrated. In a sense, integration of the total supply chain is the glue that binds the foundation for the future. The sections that follow discuss the six features of that integration: total integration, blurred boundaries, consolidation, reliability, maintenance, and economic progressiveness.

Total Integration

Total integration is an ultimate focus in which material flow is designed from the top. In other words, it is the integration of material and information flow in a true, top-down progression that begins with the customer. For example, a company that makes fiber, another company that makes fabric, yet another that dyes fabric, and one that makes dresses should all be thinking of the person planning to buy a dress.

When the ultimate customer is not the focus, the end result could be like what had happened to the fiber manufacturer that asked Tompkins to help it understand its supply chain. When asked why they wanted a study of the supply chain, the company's leaders said that a special fiber that had done really well in the early market produced a dress that customers returned after the purchase. The fiber manufacturer, the fabric maker, the dye house, the dress house, and the retailer all lost money. A Tompkins Associates analysis showed that the dress was returned because it had static cling. Had all these companies focused on the fact that customers don't like static cling and had they planned the final product accordingly, this story might have had a different conclusion. This is what I mean by anticipating a customer's need—you have to know your customer before you start making the product.

Total integration is both broad and holistic. Individual relationships are not part of this perspective because customer satisfaction is only achieved from a synthesis of the whole supply chain. Therefore, business systems are integrated. This is a logical progression that moves from Level 1 of Supply Chain Excellence to integrating internal systems to create Link Excellence at Level 2, then moves outside the organization through Visibility and ends at Level 6, the ultimate Integration. This will result in satisfying the ultimate customer. How? Here are some examples:

- Products are not being delayed on the dock because no one knows what is in the container.
- No one is reentering information that the shipping company has already entered.
- Automated advance shipping notices (ASNs) are being used.
- Crossdocking is being used.
- Inventory is being discussed with vendor management.

There are no surprises because the supply chain is truly focused on the integration of the process for the total good.

No Boundaries

By its very nature, integration shifts traditional customer/supplier and manufacturing/ warehousing boundaries during the processes of simplifying, adding value, and being responsive. The result is No Boundaries. The relationships between order entry, service, manufacturing, distribution, and other facets of a company are less defined. This also applies to external relationships. So, inside a company and out, siloism must be eliminated.

Silos were developed because they provide comfort, allowing us to say, "Well, I know my job. I am product director of this product; I am product manager on that. If I do these two things well, then I am going to succeed." Staying in a comfort zone with clearly

The Value of Total Integration — IKEA

A flow-through design maximizes handling efficiency at IKEA's distribution center (DC) in the Tejon Ranch industrial complex in Kern County, CA. The Swedish contemporary furniture company took the lessons it learned at its European DCs and combined them with new, innovative ideas to build a DC that is its only fully wireless facility and that the company now believes is its model for the future. The most noticeable characteristic of the flow-through design is a semi-automated high-bay area that uses manned storage/retrieval machines (S/RMs).

High-bay storage is not uncommon to IKEA DCs , but in the Tejon Ranch facility, the methods by which it is fed and interacts with other areas of the building are different because, unlike IKEA's European DCs, there is no rail service at Tejon Ranch. As a result, IKEA reversed the design, bringing products into the high bay near the shipping docks instead of from the receiving side of the building. This provides more efficient putaway and storage operations while saving travel distance for picking.

To maximize flow, a pallet conveyor feeds the high-bay system and crossdocks cartons, which significantly reduces heavy lift-truck traffic and travel distances. Also, Tejon's individual case-picking responds to needs for fewer products more often. Flexibility is another feature of the facility. The materials handling systems handle Euro pallets (80 x 120 centimeters) and extended IKEA pallets (80 x 200 cm). Together, they allow almost every item to be stored in racking.

Automated shipping notices (ASNs) alert the facility of impending receipts. Trailers are assigned to 30 receiving docks that run the length of the building to minimize the internal travel distance to storage. Each receipt is scanned upon arrival and the data sent to the warehouse management system (WMS). A pallet license plate is also applied and scanned. The WMS then issues a request for a lift truck or reach truck to take the load to storage. Shuttle conveyors that carry products the length of the building, scanners that read pallet license plates to determine where an item will go (or if it should be rejected), vertical lifts, and picking waves can work simultaneously to maximize movement.

Since the DC opened in 2001, IKEA has been very pleased with its performance. The building is designed to double in size to a total of 1.7 million square feet, a necessary characteristic because it will be serving additional stores and processing more SKUs in the near future. — *Modern Materials Handling,* April 2, 2002.

defined boundaries is one of the quickest paths to failure. This is a Business as Usual mindset that will take your company nowhere.

Instead, you need to use integration to move out of the comfort zone and establish your path to customer satisfaction, increased growth, and increased profitability. Consider these words from Michael Dell: "In a new, faster world, companies need to virtually integrate and cooperatively develop new technology through partnership or investments with other companies." This is the only way your company and its supply chain will get anywhere in the global marketplace.

Consolidation

The word "consolidation" brings to mind a client with 44 distribution centers that would like to reduce that number to two. However, that is only the tip of the iceberg. Industry consolidations are rising in number and speed. Financial institutions are merging globally, as are printing companies, publishing companies, telecommunications companies, and pharmaceutical companies. The results are fewer and stronger competitors, customers, and suppliers, as well as consolidation layers such as site consolidations, company consolidations, and functional consolidations, all of which may take place at the same time.

During mergers and acquisitions, consolidation often is a natural result of an action. One company buys another and eliminates clearly duplicated functions or sites. Consolidation, however, may also be the result of great effort and persistence. Efficient and effective transportation infrastructures and economies of scale that provide for higher throughput levels and customization also create consolidation. Redundancies become merely remnants or memories of the past.

Reliability

Robust systems, redundant systems, and fault-tolerant systems demand complete reliability, as do streamlined requirements, increased response time, and total inter-relatedness. The high levels of uptime these factors create make reliability even more critical.Inventory can no longer substitute for the downtime caused by unreliable processes. In turn, reliability can also cut production times and reduce failure rates. For example, an x-ray film-processing manufacturer wanted to decrease the processor assembly time. The reliability of the connectors they chose to integrate the manufacturing process eventually resulted in an assembly time of 1.5 hours instead of six. The failure rate decreased 28 percent.

Maintenance

To achieve the continuous reliability requirements that the marketplace demands, 24/7 maintenance of integrated equipment is critical, even though there will be less time and fewer people to maintain it. Therefore, preventive maintenance and predictive maintenance are key. Preventive maintenance is a continuous process, the objective of which is to minimize future maintenance problems. Predictive maintenance anticipates potential problems by sensing the operations of a machine or system and must be used to perform system self-assessment and maintenance scheduling. Preventive and predictive maintenance are not only the highest levels of maintenance, but are necessary components in achieving integration.

Economic Progressiveness

In a supply chain that has achieved Supply Chain Excellence, progressive, forward-thinking decisions are based on a total chain perspective and not on the economic justification of the individual link, plant, or department. Evolution, growth, and change are constantly taking place; therefore, all decisions we make must be based on a very broad view of the future. We need to adopt innovative practices that integrate scattered information into a whole that can be used for decision-making and demand planning, such as mining data warehouses to create data chains over the World Wide Web or exploiting the Internet to improve agility and produce savings. As Michael Dell says, "It's really a challenge of combining bits and atoms, the digital information and the physical world, and building that into every aspect of a business."

Any individual solution must be based on where we as a whole are going next; we cannot focus on a solution that is only for the here and now. Economics must be viewed progressively so that we can adapt over time.

Where Do We Go from Here?

Planning for the future requires us to move beyond the SCM approach and strive for Supply Chain Excellence. To do this, we must examine SCM to understand how it can be used as a starting point for Supply Chain Excellence. Chapter 4 will discuss the problems of SCM and demonstrate why a process must be substituted for an approach if we are to achieve Supply Chain Excellence.

The Value of Economic Progressiveness — 3M

In January 2001, James McNerney, 3M's chairman and CEO, joined the company after 18 years at GE. Shortly thereafter, McNerney introduced 3M to two initiatives—the Six Sigma process (the quality methodology created at Motorola and used at GE), and e-Productivity—as part of his plan to infuse GE-style decisiveness and profit-centered management philosophies into 3M's culture.

The Six Sigma milestones McNermey set for 3M include:

- Improved sharing of process information
- Enhanced communication of best practices
- Extension of Six Sigma from internal process to external suppliers and their suppliers
- Migration of Six Sigma across the supply chain to further reduce costs and improve quality and customer satisfaction.

Main aspects of 3M's e-Productivity initiative include:

- Requiring that technology investments demonstrate ROI, as other asset investments must
- Developing the discipline to stop operating an "old way" once capability using a "new way" is implemented, limiting costly parallel systems
- Questioning whether initiatives are stifling creativity or providing added creative time

McNerney believes that having the discipline to stop doing things the old way after technology that can provide the same capability with a different methodology has been implemented is a key element in success. "Lack of discipline is what permits parallel systems to exist for longer than they should, and this adds, rather than reduces, costs," he says.

McNerney's initiatives are already bearing profitable fruit. In April 2002, the company announced first-quarter 2002 earnings above their previously anticipated range and attributed the better-than-expected results to "accelerating benefits from Six Sigma, indirect cost reduction, and other 3M initiatives." — *Control Engineering*, October 1, 2001

NO BOUNDARIES

4

Supply Chain Management Is Not Enough

"Is it sufficient that you have learned to drive the car, or shall we look and see what is under the hood?"

— June Singer, Psychologist, Jung Institute of Chicago

Consider the following:

- 2001 was one of the worst years in the history of the electronics industry. Oversupply coupled with high inventory levels and weak equipment demand resulted in declining sales.
- Double-digit percentage declines in new-order bookings and selling prices created new tensions between metals buyers and suppliers in 2001, putting a strain on even the best supply partnerships between service centers and buyers.
- About half of all customer relationship management (CRM) projects initiated give no ROI, do not improve customer satisfaction, and are unsuccessful.
- Out-of-stock products cost the food industry $7 billion to $12 billion per year.

What does this tell us about the supply chain? The authors of a September 2001 article in *Supply Chain Management Review* made this observation: "Most supply chain managers today are stuck in what we call the 'efficiency trap'—that is, they focus inwardly on operational cost control, rather than on creating supply chain and customer service strategies to drive additional revenues."

Based on the hype that has surrounded SCM for the last 15 years, SCM should have prevented this. Why hasn't it? The answer is simple. Too many companies have implemented SCM practices and technology to do Business as Usual. This is not enough from several important perspectives—trust between a company and its suppliers, external team-work and partnerships, integration of external business process, and customer satisfaction.

What far too many supply chain managers today don't understand is that SCM is just the beginning in the process of achieving Supply Chain Excellence. It should be used as a stair step to Level 2 of the Six Levels of Supply Chain Excellence-Link Excellence. When you think about how SCM focuses on link optimization, it is easy to see that this is true.

So, why have so many managers and company leaders missed the boat when trying to implement SCM? There are various reasons: the original philosophy behind SCM, the fact that it is treated as an approach and not a process, the issue of alliances, the growth of build-to-order (BTO), the fact that SCM is a logistics concept, and a lack of understanding that SCM is only the beginning. These reasons are discussed in this chapter.

The Original SCM Philosophy

The original philosophy behind SCM was, "If I build it, the orders will come." It can be broken down into three parts:

1. *Supply*—indicates a push
2. *Chain*—indicates individual, discrete links
3. *Management*—implies a static environment of control and measurement.

Problems are inherent in all three. "Push" no longer gets the job done, because it gives control to suppliers rather than the ultimate customer. Viewing the supply chain as indi-vidual links is also problematic. Like the practice of medicine a century ago, it treats symptoms but does not try to discover a cause. For example, optimizing warehouse management without taking into account other elements, such as sourcing and purchasing, production and inventory planning, transportation and distribution, and customer satisfac-tion probably will not yield the desired results. The source of the warehousing problems may not actually be a function of warehouse management, but something else entirely. As for "management," the static, controlled environment implied by the term also suggests containment. A healthy, flowing supply chain is not contained; it cannot be, for that would make it resistant to change.

The original SCM philosophy, then, is one of push, links, and containment. Such a philosophy cannot succeed in a marketplace that demands a combination of pull and push (not just push), flow (not links), and harnessing (not containing) the energy of change. It does not supply the speed, flexibility, modularity, unselfishness, agility, and synchronization necessary in today's global and technological marketplace. It is no longer viable in this burgeoning, BTO, quick-response world—a world with No Boundaries. Unfortunately, many of the companies that have tried to succeed with SCM have done so based on its original philosophy and without regard to how it has changed as the marketplace has changed.

Approach, Not Process

What do Efficient Healthcare Response (EHCR), Efficient Consumer Response (ECR), Efficient Foodstuff Response (EFR), Quick Response (QR), Just-In-Time (JIT), Continuous Flow Distribution, and SCM have in common? They are all approaches. At one time, each has been viewed as the answer to high inventory, high costs, and growing customer dissatisfaction. None has worked. Most have or will be discarded. Why? Again, because they are all approaches.

The problem with approaches is that they are not open-ended. Companies implement them once and expect results. They grasp at the approaches, but do not try to understand or maintain them for long periods of time. Today's challenges require processes, not approaches. Processes are open-ended. They shift, they change, they can be adjusted, and they flow. You can take a process at any point, review it, alter it, and improve it. You are not given that opportunity with approaches.

Those who use SCM for Business as Usual view it as an approach that looks at a link with the aim of optimizing it. From this perspective, it does not robustly address change. It assumes that there is no marketplace turbulence and that links may be optimized independently of the rate of change. Any company that tries to optimize links while ignoring change will face failure.

The Issue of Alliances

SCM does not encourage alliances and partnerships outside the individual link. As a rule, executives do not see suppliers as partners. In a May 20, 1999, article in Purchasing magazine, Anne Millen wrote what a lot of organizations were thinking at the time: Close relationships, and their subsequent sharing of strategic information, led to kickbacks, insider trading, and a sense of owning the vendor's time, product, and resources. SCM does not provide the means for overcoming mistrust or creating new partnership models.

Happily, the fears of a few years ago may have abated somewhat. A 2002 survey of 150 Fortune 1000 executives revealed that most of them believed creative partnering agreements might prove vital to supply chain success. About 70 percent of the survey respondents said they foresaw partnerships moving beyond the traditional material agreements to new models.

BTO

Build-to-Order (BTO) is a pull methodology in which customer needs are considered first and then the products are manufactured. BTO is the ultimate synchronization of supply to demand. How big is BTO? As Cisco Systems and Dell Computers find competitive advantage in their BTO philosophy, many other OEMs are divesting themselves of manufacturing operations altogether, paving the way for CEMs, both big niche players and smaller firms, to prosper. "Build-to-order infrastructure can offer numerous benefits such as cost and inventory reduction, customer retention, and maximized margins," says Brad Perkins, a senior director for Oracle Asia-Pacific.

BTO has been the norm in the electronics and computer industries since the 1990s, but it isn't just for Dell anymore. Companies that do not need to fill a vast consumer distribution chain and whose buyers—whether they are individuals or clients—demand customization or special features are relying on BTO. Most of these companies do not practice BTO exclusively, but it is making inroads into most industries in some fashion.

So, what does BTO bring these companies? Customer satisfaction, reduced costs, higher profits, shorter cycle times, much smaller inventories, reduced work in process, much quicker inventory turns, and agility are the usual results of BTO. In the Internet age, these are more than benefits; they are requirements. Now, other industries are flirting with it, including automakers Nissan and Mazda and telecommunications companies Lucent and Nortel. Both Ford and GM are investigating the possibilities of BTO to sell customized cars online. GM has also completed a study of what would be necessary for the company to take orders online, custom-produce the products, and deliver them on a promised date.

"There is a tidal wave of opportunity," says Michael Marks, the CEO of Flextronics. SCM does not allow companies to ride this wave. It is a push methodology, one built on the premise that products should be manufactured first and orders fulfilled second. Again, this is because SCM was not invented to adjust to such a big change in manufacturing methodology.

A Logistics Concept

SCM is a logistics concept. Logistics is defined as an organization's internal coordination of management of raw material, material flow through production, and the physical distribution of finished goods. In other words, logistics begins with a company's need to order raw materials and ends when the finished goods are shipped. Change or turbulence in the supply chain from either suppliers or customers is viewed as a major irritant and efforts are put forth to minimize the effects.

Basically, logistics is within a link. Therefore, it is not surprising that SCM looks upstream and downstream, but only to improve the performance of the individual link. There is no continuous improvement of the whole supply chain, as SCM is not a supply chain concept, but a link and logistics concept.

SCM Is Just the Beginning

Optimizing each link in the supply chain is only the beginning. If an organization hopes to pursue Supply Chain Excellence, it must first look within itself, eliminate any boundaries between departments and facilities, operate as a single entity working toward the same goals, and begin a never-ending journey of continuous improvement. The result is Link Excellence. No organization should even begin to think about Supply Chain Excellence until it has achieved Link Excellence.

Some Link Excellence initiatives can benefit from logistics and SCM. However, it is important that companies recognize that SCM and logistics prin-

OEMs and CEMs

After expanding revenues to $83 billion in 2000 from $47 billion in 1999, the top 50 CEMs saw revenues decline in 2001. However, over the longer term, the outlook for the electronics contract manufacturing industry appears bright. Purchasing's 2001 annual survey of those companies indicated that many have boosted their capabilities. For example, the leading CEMS—Solectron, Celestica, and Flextronics— have started acquiring their customers' production facilities.

These purchases allow CEMs to increase capacity while the OEMs eliminate facilities expenses and improve profits without sacrificing the quality of the manufactured products. Furthermore, the CEMs can design and build complete systems that are shipped directly to the end customer. Some CEMs also offer repair services on the products they build, permitting the OEMs to battle time-to-market and price pressures.

According to a study completed by Bear, Stearns and Co., the total available market for contract manufacturing was $500 billion. Less than 20 percent of the electronics manufacturing market was being outsourced, which means that there is tremendous room for future growth in this area. — *Purchasing*, October 18, 2001

Logistics for Supply Chain Excellence: *Verizon Logistics*

Verizon Logistics' Westfield, Ind., National Logistics Center is Verizon's supply chain link to phone technicians in Indiana and five neighboring states, other company-owned regional logistics centers, and commercial customers nationwide. The center distributes phone sets, caller ID units, DSL circuits, coils of wire, and a host of other products. The company upgraded the Indiana facility with pick-to-light processing in a multi-level pick module, a sliding shoe sorter, and a warehouse management system (WMS). The facility redesign has improved split-case processing productivity, increased throughput without adding labor, and consolidated in-house inventories.

The process starts when carriers deliver products to Westfield's 14 receiving docks. A worker removes the packing slip from each incoming carton and keys it into a nearby terminal to notify the WMS of its arrival. Putaway labels for each carton or pallet are scanned so that the WMS can determine a storage location in the bulk floor area, very narrow aisle (VNA) pallet rack storage, or the pick module.

Items for the bulk floor storage are taken by lift truck to areas located on both sides of the DC. Most of these are high-volume movers that can be stacked several pallets high. Also stored here are oversized items. Full pallets and individual cartons are stored in the VNA racks. Lift trucks carry loads to pick up and delivery stations at the ends of the VNA aisles. The WMS then directs putaway narrow-aisle trucks with onboard wireless terminals.

Order fulfillment is in waves based on specific carrier delivery routes. Most pallet and full-case picks are performed for telephone company customers, the regional logistic centers, and commercial clients.

After the upgrade, pick rates increased 260 percent. In the past year, operating costs of the center declined an additional 29 percent from the upgraded facility's already lower numbers. A large component of that resulted from reduced overtime and temporary labor costs, which fell nearly 36 percent as picks per hour per employee increased 25 percent. — *Modern Materials Handling*, April 1, 2002 ciples are merely tools, neither of which will take them beyond Link Excellence. To do that, continuous improvement initiatives are necessary, and their most critical objective is organizational readiness for Supply Chain Excellence.

Ready, Set, Go!: Moving Beyond SCM

To deliver maximum value, customization, and satisfaction to the ultimate customer while at the same time reducing inventory, trimming lead times, and reducing costs, all the links in the supply chain must be integrated, synthesized, and synchronized to function as a single entity. The goal of this entity should be to satisfy the ultimate customer by anticipating his or her needs and expectations. No longer can the business mentality be "my company versus your company." In today's marketplace, the thinking is "my supply chain versus your supply chain."

If a supply chain does not satisfy its ultimate customer, each link, one by one, will go out of business by default. This is a hard fact, but it is a reality. Keen business minds will see the opportunity in the challenge and readily shift their thinking to a total supply chain with No Boundaries so that they may individually and collectively prosper. This means taking what they can from SCM to improve their links and then moving beyond it.

5

The Supply Chain Excellence Opportunity

"If you go slow, you will fall."

— Chris Stewart, Off-road Motorcycle Champion

So much has occurred with my view of the supply chain that it is almost unbelievable. I want to put this in a context so you can catch up with where we are and where the supply chain is going. Then, I'll present the exciting opportunities of Supply Chain Excellence.

Historical Framework

Consider the history of technology: First there was the wheel, then the Industrial Revolution, electricity, the Machine Age, the fork truck, the conveyor, and the computer. Yet, none of these accomplishments gives us a framework within which we can discuss where the supply chain is today. A better framework would be to consider the history of my growth; specifically, how I came to understand integration and how the concept of Supply Chain Excellence came to be.

Beyond Worker and Workplace

The first time I believed I understood the topic of integration was in 1966. I was taking a course in work methods at Purdue University. I knew that the worker and the workplace had to be integrated. Alone, the worker and workplace were individual elements. However, when someone combined them in an ergonomic way, the result was something special. I can recall very clearly my thought at the time, which was, "This is something I can grab onto. I now have an awareness of worker and workplace that I did not have before. This is exciting."

Then, a few years later, I worked as an intern under former President Nixon in Washington, DC. I worked on problems with the Post Office, and I began to understand that there was more to integration than worker and workplace. Conveyors were also involved. I soon realized their impact; changing the speed and changing the load being moved created an interaction that required an integrated, mechanical material handling equipment solution.

In the early 1970s, my thought processes changed once again. I focused on the worker, the workstation, material handling equipment, and how the computer controlled the work environment. The integrated material handling equipment grew into a material handling system. Then I understood that there was more to it than just this system. I had to combine all the moves of the warehouse and the factory and develop a system that handled the totality of distribution and the totality of manufacturing. So, in 1974, I wrote my first paper on material handling systems and the importance of implementing them correctly.

In 1978, a client hired Tompkins Associates to implement a material handling system design in Texas. We designed the facility with automated guided vehicles, automated storage and retrieval, and state-of-the-art conveyor sortation. After the system was installed, I stood there on ribbon-cutting day and heard how efficient the system was. But I thought, "This is not quality work." I realized then that what matters is not how well the material handling system works, but instead how well the factory and the DC work. It was not about material handling systems, but rather manufacturing systems and distribution systems.

The Supply Chain

My realization at that ribbon-cutting ceremony shaped my perspective until the early 1980s. When SCM came into being, I took a hard look at it. I saw that SCM looks upstream and downstream with the objective of optimizing individual links, but it soon became clear to me that SCM was not the ultimate supply chain process. I found that optimized links were not enough; I was interested in optimal chains. I also decided that "optimization" really was not the best word choice.

"Optimization," by definition, indicates a predetermined objective function that must be maximized or minimized. We cannot optimize a supply chain today because of the rate at which supply chains evolve. What we should strive for is to have the best for that specific moment through agility, but we must also focus on continuous improvement over time. That is where we are today. We need to synthesize the chain until there are No Boundaries, and then we have to go one step further—to accelerated synchronization. I view it like this: I see the big chain passing over the flame of synthesis, the flame melting the chain and creating a flow of molten metal that moves smoothly. This flow creates a world of opportunity for us.

The Supply Chain Opportunity

When he took on the task of redesigning his division's supply chain, Dave Tronnes, Director of Manufacturing Administration for the Toner Products Division of Toshiba, realized he had to address these supply chain trends:

• Fewer supplies
• Increased focus on customer satisfaction
• Purchasers driving shorter cycle times
• A greater role for design engineers on the sourcing team
• Increased global sourcing
• Increased single sourcing
• Greater emphasis on strategic alliances with suppliers
• Elimination of non-value-added supply chain activities
• An increased role for purchasing professionals in strategic decision-making
• Operational changes in the business process

His goals included

• Lower purchase prices
• Lower transportation costs
• Reduced lead times on materials and supplies
• Higher quality supplies
• Increased profits and reduced (or unchanged) travel
• Increased communications capabilities through systems improvement

How interesting. Tronnes noticed the same trends I have. His goals, based on these trends, are admirable. The opportunities presented to us by Supply Chain Excellence are quite similar to Tronnes's goals. Supply Chain Excellence will:

• Increase return on assets (ROA)
• Improve customer satisfaction
• Maximize speed

Inventory Management — Tarrant Apparel

Tarrant Apparel Group, a leading provider of private-label casual clothing, saw fourth quarter 2001 profits soar over those of 2000. The company attributes this to effective inventory management brought about by working closely with their customers and rapidly producing and delivering high-quality, fashionable merchandise in an efficient and timely manner. They also vertically integrated their Mexican operations so that they could align their manufacturing processes with their customers' shift in buying patterns.

The company was committed to maintaining lmoderate spending levels, and, as a result, its year-over-year operating expenses decreased significantly. According to Gerard Guez, Chairman and CEO of Tarrant, "We remain optimistic about our future growth potential following an eventual turnaround in market conditions. Since our current capacity is more than sufficient to support long-term rapid growth, we will be able to leverage our cutting-edge production capabilities."

— *BusinessWire,* March 19, 2002

- Reduce costs
- Integrate the supply chain

Let's take a closer look at each of these.

Increase ROA

Supply Chain Excellence increases ROA by maximizing inventory turns, minimizing obsolete inventory, maximizing employee participation, and maximizing continuous improvement. Traditionally, companies have tried to increase ROA by increasing the turns of the fast-moving products. This actually nets minimal impact. Often the challenge is not the fast-moving product, but the slow-moving one. In most cases, the focus should not be on the most popular items, but on the slow-moving and obsolete inventory.

"Employees are a company's most valuable asset." How often have we heard that? Although it may seem that it is said far too often, in reality, it is not said enough. It tends to be lost among profit and loss calculations, and it should not be. When a company begins viewing its employees as assets, then that company can begin to maximize their participation in its operations and its successes. An effective means of maximizing employee participation is to realize the value of their intellectual capital. Knowledge is such a prized commodity in today's marketplace that many employees are now being called "knowledge workers." Companies should capitalize on this asset, while also making sure that their employees have been provided with the tools to harness the energy of change and adapt to its results with agility.

Continuous improvement is one of the most effective ways to maximize employee participation. If a company and its employees constantly look for ways to improve the entire supply chain and realize that nothing in this world is finite, then that company and its supply chain will achieve the ultimate goal: Supply Chain Excellence.

Improve Customer Satisfaction

Customer satisfaction is the output of Supply Chain Excellence. It is also the means by which the effectiveness of a supply chain is measured. Customer satisfaction means being easy to do business with, fulfilling promises to customer, and responding to customer needs. In other words, it is an ongoing, escalating process of meeting requirements and exceeding expectations.

Supply Chain Excellence creates companies that respond to the customer's needs through customization and that use data-mining applications to exploit data warehouses to create a data chain. They understand value-added activity. They also understand the need for agility and the need to meet ever-changing customer requirements. They completely comprehend the meaning of high quality and strive to provide high value.

Mass Customization — Reflect.com

Companies in several industries have announced or completed mass-customization projects. Major players in the auto industry are experimenting with customization offers. Nike lets customers choose the color, material, cushioning, and other attributes for athletic shoes. With Reflect.com, which is backed by Proctor & Gamble, women can create and order custom personal-care products.

Reflect.com customers answer a long questionnaire about their personal-care preferences. The company uses this information to develop customized makeup, perfume, and hair-care and skin-care products, which are then shipped directly to the customer. It also sends out customized e-mail newsletters based on the information each customer provides. — *ZDNet Tech Update, October 1, 2001 and December 24, 2001*

Maximize Speed

As I think about the demands for speed, I see a direct correlation between them and a lesson I learned when my son and I took up off-road motorcycle riding in 1998. By May 1999, he had ridden quite a bit and was pretty good. I, however, had ridden approximately

10 hours, and my proficiency did not approach his. Undaunted by this difference, I agreed when he suggested we participate in an off-road trip in the Sequoia National Forest he had discovered on the Internet.

We flew to California and met our tour group, which consisted of national champions; young, strong riders; great riders; and Jimmy and me. Jimmy proved to be a natural and was soon going up and down the mountains with the best riders. I was another story. I was 20 years older than the other riders, I was 12,000 feet above sea level, I had 10 hours of motorcycle experience, and I was in the mountains.

After the first day, Chris Stewart, a three-time, national off-road motorcycle champion, sat down with me and made three observations:

1. He was a more experienced motorcycle rider than I was.
2. He knew the mountains and had more experience riding off-road than I had.
3. He had fallen off a motorcycle more than I had and had many more broken bones and injuries as a result of these falls than I did.

Having established his credibility, he then said, "Ride fast! If you go slow, you will fall. The steeper the incline, the bumpier the road, then the faster you must ride or you will fall."

"If you go slow, you will fall," applies equally to business as it does to off-road motorcycle riding. Companies, particularly those traveling over steep inclines and bumpy roads, must be able to "ride fast" to do BTO, to respond to the customer, to be quick. A company that strives to achieve Supply Chain Excellence will be able to do this, as well as fill orders quickly. That company will see response times and lead times reduced, and it will respond quickly to the marketplace. Why? Because Supply Chain Excellence allows—through partnerships, communication, distribution synthesis, and manufacturing synthesis—the design of multilevel networks. These networks are complex entities comprising several partnerships, some of which may involve outsourcing and third-party firms. They are also agile, meeting a range of customer satisfaction requirements. Robust design methods enabled by real-time decision tools and demand planning are the source of this agility.

For example, a company used a multilevel network to meet the demands of two large companies with long lead-times and those of small, regional firms that needed products delivered within 24 hours. The company created three full-stocking DCs, then set up multiple crossdocks near the small companies for fast-moving products.

Reduce Costs

Supply Chain Excellence is about providing higher customer satisfaction and providing greater value while reducing supply chain costs and thus growing the supply chain profitability. Companies must reduce costs or their supply chains will fail. Industry publications are filled with articles on how to reduce costs and stories about companies that have reduced costs, but where are the articles on reducing costs within the supply chain? Did a company's cost reductions result in the supply chain meeting customer requirements at a lower cost? Cost reductions within a link are only of value if they also reduce costs in the supply chain. Transportation costs, acquisition costs, distribution costs, inventory carrying costs, reverse logistics costs, packaging costs, etc., must all be scrutinized to assure that significantly lower supply chain costs are achieved, then further reduced. Cost reductions of 2 percent, 5 percent, or even 10 percent are not significant. Significant cost reductions may start at about 20 percent, but ideally, they should range from 40 percent to 60 percent.

The attitude and approach of someone attempting to reduce costs by 5 percent is totally different from the attitude and approach of someone attempting a 50 percent cost reduction. Five percent

Maximizing Speed — Soligen Technologies

Soligen Technologies, Inc., a rapid manufacturer of cast metal parts, rapidly produces three-dimensional ceramic casting molds directly from computer-aided design (CAD) files, shaving weeks off production time for cast metal parts. Soligen's Direct Shell Production Casting (DSPC(r)) technology allows the company to bypass the traditional need for tooling. This technology is a proprietary fabrication process for metal parts that produces ceramic molds for metal castings directly from the CAD file. Consequently, it enables postponement of design and the fabrication of expensive and time-consuming casting tooling until after the parts are functionally tested, thus increasing the probability of making production tooling correctly on the first attempt.

Additionally, Soligen rapidly produces production tooling for larger runs of metal castings from the same CAD file as the approved part. By combining three key production elements: DSPC technology, conventional casting methods, and Computerized Numerical Control (CNC) machining practices, the company has created the first "one-stop shop" for ready-to-assemble functional metal parts made directly from a CAD file. — *Automotive Design and Production,* September 2001 and Soligen Press release, June 5, 2001 reductions are the result of something simple, such as installing software that reduces paperwork. Fifty percent reductions require dynamic consistency and include eliminating waste and redundancy while practicing continuous improvement throughout the supply chain. This takes innovation, perseverance, and the ability to see the solution after next.

Integrate the Supply Chain

Supply Chain Excellence is all about using partnerships and communication to synchronize the demands of the customers with the supply of the supply chain. The supply chain is integrated and focused on the ultimate customer; its links work together in true partnerships. In other words, each link cares more about the supply chain than it does about itself because it has realized that its individual success is based upon the success of the chain. This synchronization demands a new level of communication that is truly real-time and instantaneous throughout the supply chain. This synchronization of links and communications characterizes Supply Chain Excellence and will provide the oneness required for the supply chain to respond quickly as a single entity to the challenges and opportunities of tomorrow.

Make It Happen

In summary, supply chains that adopt a synthesized approach are going to have major successes. Organizations that do not move beyond SCM will fail. To make Supply Chain Excellence happen, it is important to be armed with that knowledge as well as the realization that there will be resistance to it. Executives will say, "I don't need to do this because none of my competition is doing it."

The answer to such objections is a quote from Yogi Berra, who said, "If you come to a fork in the road, take it." And that's what I say to you. Seize the initiative. Make Supply Chain Excellence happen. The following chapters will show you how.

6

The Characteristics of Supply Chain Excellence and What It Is Not

"One cannot do right in one department of life whilst he is occupied in doing wrong in any other department. Life is an individual whole."

— Gandhi

A U.S. Bancorp Piper Jaffray report released in December 2001 had this to say about integration: "In the mid-1980s, integrated supply came to the forefront as a new concept."

This is amazing, when you think about it. Even though someone has known since the 1980s how important integration of the supply chain is, logistics and supply chain professionals have focused on link optimization, not integration of the supply chain. When a voice like U.S. Bancorp Piper Jaffray comes along and pronounces, "Dramatic savings are a very real benefit when an integrated supply program is properly implemented," then suddenly, out of the blue, supply chain professionals are saying, "We have to do it."

The professionals may have come to their realization because logistics and SCM are not serving to integrate and synchronize the supply chain. The supply chain integration that interests these professionals, along with other company executives can be accomplished by achieving Supply Chain Excellence. This chapter examines the differences among Supply Chain Excellence, logistics, and SCM; describes the five characteristics of Supply Chain Excellence; discusses what it is not; and introduces the eight core competencies necessary for achieving Supply Chain Excellence.

Logistics

Logistics focuses on the internal coordination of materials management (raw materials), material flow through production (work in progress), and physical distribution (finished goods). In other words, logistics begins with the need to order raw materials and ends when the finished goods are shipped. Change is viewed as a major irritant and efforts are put forth to minimize the effects. Historically, logistics has never looked at true integration or the issue of using the energy of change to create agility; its focus is internal.

SCM

SCM is a logistics approach to integrating many links of the supply chain by optimizing each link while attempting to control change. A commonly accepted definition is "the delivery of enhanced customer and economic value through synchronized management of the flow of physical goods from sourcing to consumption." In reality, the way SCM is practiced is to view the flow of physical goods from sourcing to consumption within a link of the chain. While it can be used as a tool to start the process of achieving Supply Chain Excellence, SCM does not acknowledge that the supply chain is a whole and therefore must be viewed holistically.

SCM is a step beyond logistics because it maintains that it is unacceptable to view logistics as an individual link. SCM emphasizes that the integration of many links in the supply chain is important and will eliminate waste. However, the focus of SCM is the optimization of each link to ensure the proper supply to links further down the supply chain. SCM asserts that change must be managed, which can be translated as "controlled." In the SCM philosophy, controlling all deviations from the original plan theoretically allows link optimization to contribute to the optimization of the whole supply chain.

In addition to this link optimization challenge, the SCM philosophy that change can be managed and controlled is without foundation. Change cannot be managed or controlled.

Supply Chain Excellence

To achieve Supply Chain Excellence, the supply chain must have in place a holistic, continuous improvement process of ensuring customer satisfaction from the original raw material provider to the ultimate finished product consumer. The supply chain is synthesized because the links are integrated, unified, synchronized, and brought together as a whole.

Supply Chain Excellence has No Boundaries. It also recognizes that competition in today's marketplace is supply chain vs. supply chain and that sometimes companies that once were like fighting siblings are now allies in the battle between supply chains.

Just as SCM picks up where logistics leaves off, Supply Chain Excellence picks up where SCM leaves off. While SCM results in link excellence, Supply Chain Excellence results in the synthesis and synchronization of the total integrated pipeline from a customer perspective. Also, where SCM implies a static, controlled environment, the supply chain that has achieved Supply Chain Excellence harnesses the energy of change to address the turbulence of the marketplace with agility and achieve true continuous improvement.

What we have, then, is a progression of thought and corresponding improvements of performance from logistics to SCM to Supply Chain Excellence. Performance does improve when a move is made from logistics to SCM. However, performance improves even more after a move beyond SCM. The five characteristics of Supply Chain Excellence discussed below help explain why.

Well-defined Process

Achieving Supply Chain Excellence is a well-defined process that is understood by all links along the supply chain. It aligns the complete supply chain. For example, if only two links of the supply chain are pursuing excellence, the chain cannot be expected to net the same results that would occur if the entire supply chain were aligned and synchronized. Links A and B may have learned the benefits of integration and, as a result, gained competitive advantage. If they do not communicate with, integrate, and synchronize links C and D, however, the overall supply chain will not gain the advantage.

Those who strive to achieve Supply Chain Excellence will see that it is important to consider every aspect of the supply chain and understand how each process fits, interacts, and integrates. Otherwise, critical information will be lost or an important link will be missing and all will be lost. An excellent analogy is the historic Y2K scare. No matter how much money was spent on upgrading computer systems so that they were Y2K compliant, the failure of one little chip somewhere could have brought down power grids, telecommunications systems, and banking systems. Those who wrote the files to ready systems for Y2K had to keep this fact in mind, and you must do the same when pursuing Supply Chain Excellence.

Integrated Process

For more than 15 years, the supply chain focus has been on optimizing links. That's selfish. It can be compared to stealing the basketball from your own teammates so that you can score the winning goal. A team needs all players to work together to win a ball game. Even Michael Jordan, in his early days with the Bulls, couldn't win games alone despite his high scoring. He needed teamwork. When the rest of the team realized the importance of teamwork, the Bulls became NBA champions in 1991, 1992, and 1993.

Achieving Supply Chain Excellence is an integrated process in which selfishness is not allowed. This includes eliminating silos and focusing all links on customer satisfaction. To eliminate silos, we synthesize the whole, from the original link to the ultimate customer, and ensure that all links are synchronized. That's how all links become focused on continuous improvement of the chain. When this is achieved, we have created a supply chain with No Boundaries.

Harnessing the Energy of Change

Pursuing Supply Chain Excellence is a process in which the total pipeline understands the energy of change and has a desire to harness this energy to create the agility necessary for ensuring competitive advantage. This involves courage and innovation. By harnessing change, we can turn it into agility—an asset for the total supply chain. Instead of thinking, "I want to improve my link," you may have to think, "Tradeoffs within my link might be what are needed to improve the supply chain."

To many companies, such thinking is inconceivable. They believe that making a tradeoff for the sake of the supply chain can only bring ruin because they are compromising competitive advantage. That might be true in some cases, but when a company has the success of its total supply chain in mind, its tradeoffs will result in a win. To illustrate this point, I'll return to Michael Jordan. Sports fans think of him as being the one who shot the winning basket in most games, but the beauty of Michael Jordan as a player is the fact that he also recognizes when a teammate had a better chance of scoring than he and passes the ball. For the sake of the win, he will give up the ball. Michael is a true competitor and knows that there is plenty of glory for all in getting the win. Sometimes you have to give up your link perspective for the sake of the chain and the sake of the win.

No Information Delays

Supply Chain Excellence does not accept information delays. It requires true partnerships, synchronization, and an integration of information throughout the supply chain—the result of two of the Six Levels of Supply Chain Excellence: Visibility (Level 3) and Collaboration (Level 4). If a link is slowing information flow, it must be removed from the chain and replaced with an alternative. Otherwise, agility is lost.

Communication delays are as bad as siloism. To meet increasing demands for speed, we not only need organizations to do the right thing, we also need each organization to let all other links know quickly what it is doing. The adage, "The chain is only as strong as its weakest link," becomes, "Synthesis is only as quick as its slowest link." Communication becomes key.

With SCM, the progression of knowledge is linear. One link talks to another, which talks to the next, which talks to the next, and so forth. It is similar to the game of Gossip —the one in which the first person in a group whispers something into a neighbor's ear and the second person whispers to the third and on until the end, when the last person says out loud what he heard. Inevitably, that phrase is a mutant form of the original message.

With Supply Chain Excellence, thanks to Visibility and Collaboration, the entire chain communicates simultaneously. Linearity has disappeared and in its place is robust and simultaneous communication via the Internet. Without accuracy and speed in communications, Supply Chain Excellence is impossible. For a supply chain to achieve Supply Chain Excellence, the supply chain must synchronize the demands of the customer with the supply in the chain in as close to real time as possible. Therefore, communication is a core competency of Supply Chain Excellence. Anything that delays communication along the supply chain must be eliminated or replaced.

Supply Chain Performance

Partnerships are critical in the pursuit of Supply Chain Excellence, not only link-to-link, but in the total supply chain. Achieving Supply Chain Excellence is a continuous improvement process with the criteria presented in Chapter 5—ROA, customer satisfaction, speed, costs, and integration. Because the supply chain focuses on these five performance criteria, competitive advantage and true Supply Chain Excellence will be achieved.

What These Characteristics Demonstrate

The characteristics of Supply Chain Excellence demonstrate that it is not SCM. SCM is an approach focused on link optimization and it best serves the supply chain when it is used to achieve Link Excellence, the starting point for Supply Chain Excellence. SCM is not a process; it clearly has boundaries. Supply Chain Excellence also is not Demand Chain Management, Demand Network Management, Demand Network Integration, Value Chain Management, or Customer-Driven Demand Network; nor is it Supply Chain Coordination, Supply Chain Integration, or Demand/Supply Chain Management. These are all names for link approaches rather than for a holistic process. The section that follows describes these

The Value of Crossdocking

Crossdocking is receiving and processing goods for reshipping in the shortest time possible, with minimum handling and no storage time. It is a practice that has proven ROI. The beauty of the crossdocking methodology is also that it is not industry-specific: Wholesalers love it for pushing time-sensitive, fast-moving, sale, and promotional merchandise. Distributors use it to consolidate freight; general and retail distribution is enhanced, especially when door-to-store transport is possible (i.e., an outbound trailer at the shipping dock for each store serviced by the facility).

Crossdocking obviously benefits the single link, but how does it benefit the entire supply chain? Think in terms of handling costs. Less handling means more accuracy, less probability of product damage, less wear on material handling equipment, and less labor. The supply chain is paying less and assuming less risk with every SKU crossdocked. Ultimately, however, think in terms of customer responsiveness. You're effectively bypassing storage and order-picking and going directly to shipping. How much more responsive can you be? Crossdocking provides the ultimate in speed and agility through links of the supply chain. That supports synchronization of customer demands and the supply chain's supply.

linear approaches and compares them with Supply Chain Excellence.

The Limits of Where We Have Been

Demand Chain Management handles order management, distribution logistics, inventory replenishment, and demand planning. Like SCM, its focus is the link; it looks downstream and focuses on only the demand aspect of the supply chain. Demand Network Management is similar to Demand Chain Management, except that it has a marketing component that may or may not contribute to the competitive advantage of the supply chain.

Demand Network Integration is similar to Demand Network Management, but it is broader in that it has a greater real-time response to changes in demand. The same may be said for Customer-Driven Demand Network, but it has a greater awareness of the build-to-order and customization requirements that exist downstream. The Value Chain Management mindset goes a bit further in that it desires to look both at the demand and supply requirements of the supply chain. Unfortunately, Value Chain Management is still an approach, not a process, pursuing optimization instead of meeting the true needs of continuous improvement.

At first glance, Supply Chain Coordination is alluring. Coordination is an integral component of supply chain design. Well-coordinated, discrete activities are more efficient than disjointed, independent actions. But, Supply Chain Coordination still allows the slowest or weakest link to determine overall operating efficiency and speed of the supply chain. Most importantly, Supply Chain Coordination does not mean Supply Chain Integration, and it is based upon link optimization.

Declaring that Supply Chain Integration is not Supply Chain Excellence may seem confusing when you consider how I have been emphasizing how important Integration is to achieving Supply Chain Excellence. The important thing to remember is that there is no one solution for achieving Supply Chain Excellence. Integration alone cannot take a supply chain to the pinnacle. Also, although Supply Chain Integration is viewed as producing greater technological innovation, leveraged knowledge, shared business risks, shorter cycle times (both production and design), and integration of production planning, it does not provide the tools for harnessing change and creating agility.

Demand/Supply Chain Management is similar to Value Chain Management in that it combines what are seen as traditional supply components (e.g., purchasing, inventory management, MES, MRP, and process control) with what are seen as traditional demand components (e.g., demand management,

Collaborative Integration Is Growing

IT is finally beginning to live up to its promises, and a few manufacturers, their suppliers and their customers are now effectively collaborating by merging their systems to share product designs and specifications, demand forecasts, production status, inventory information, and order and shipment data. According to *IndustryWeek*'s 2002 Value-Chain Survey, several manufacturers have gained a competitive advantage by breaking down functional walls within their organizations, nurturing collaborative relationships with business partners and investing in communication links to more rapidly convey customer needs and desires. In fact, several of those manufacturers responding to the 2002 Value-Chain Survey confirmed that what were once viewed as pie-in-the sky dreams of transparency, real-time information flow and profit-enhancing business partnerships are now becoming increasingly real. *IndustryWeek* views this as a positive trend and predicts that more and more companies, now that they've realized the value of collaborative integration, will adopt its practices. — IndustryWeek.com, April 1, 2002 planning, scheduling, sales, order fulfillment). Like SCM, Demand/Supply Chain Management is a logistics concept, and it still focuses on link optimization.

No Boundaries

SCM, Demand Change Management, Demand Network Management, Demand Network Integration, Customer-Driven Demand Network, Value Chain Management, Supply Chain Coordination, Supply Chain Integration, and Demand/Supply Chain Management all share one characteristic: Every one of these approaches has boundaries. Supply Chain Excellence replaces these boundaries with partnerships, not only link-to-link, but in the total chain. A successful supply chain has No Boundaries.

Eight Core Competencies

Changing the way your business works is a challenge. Supply Chain Excellence can meet that challenge. The eight core competencies necessary for Supply Chain Excellence can help. These eight core competencies are:

1. Agility
2. Peak-to-Peak Performance
3. Customer Satisfaction
4. Supply Chain Holism
5. Manufacturing Synthesis
6. Distribution Synthesis
7. Partnerships
8. Communications.

These eight competencies are the subject of the next eight chapters.

7

Agility

"Adapt or perish, now as ever, is Nature's inexorable imperative."
— H.G. Wells

Lefty Gomez was one of the greatest pitchers in the history of the New York Yankees. In 1934, for example, he won 26 games and lost only five. However, as time went on, he lost his edge.

Joe McCarthy, the Yankees' manager, counseled him. "I don't think you're throwing as hard as you need to."

Lefty replied, "You're wrong, Joe. I'm throwing twice as hard. But the ball isn't going as fast."

That's exactly what is happening in business today. Companies are working hard—very hard—but the product doesn't flow as fast as it should. What ails these companies is not change per se, but the fact that they try to manage change without understanding this point: you cannot manage change, but you can harness its energy to become agile and reap the benefits. This chapter discusses why you cannot manage change, discusses the science of change and how to harness its energy to create agility, and explains why agility is one of the eight core competencies required to achieve Supply Chain Excellence.

You Cannot Manage Change

Change, despite the declarations of many business leaders and writers, is not manageable. Organizations can attempt to drive markets and customers in a specific direction, but the climate of commerce is as unpredictable as next week's weather. Managing change cannot be accomplished. You can ride the wave of change, but you cannot tell the wave how high or challenging it must be.

Not long ago, a flyer that advertised a seminar on managing change appeared on my desk. Curious, I picked it up and looked for a picture of God, for only God can manage or

Sears — A Story of Resistance

For the 12 years (1980-1992) that he was CEO of Sears, Ed Brennan instituted a number of changes that should have been profitable. He sold the Sears Tower, instituted the acceptance of other credit cards along with the Sears credit card, launched Brand Central, diversified into financial services, and invested a great deal to launch the Discover Card. He also simplified logistics, focused on selling women's apparel, began streamlining the buying organization, and created specialized Sears automotive, home-furnishing, and home-improvement stores.

Unfortunately, it is Brennan's successor, Arthur Martinez, who is well-known for revitalizing the retail side of Sears. Why? Because Brennan failed to understand the pain of change and the resistance it can create. Store management teams, upset and angry about layoffs, decentralization, and threats of more layoffs, alienated customers with their inconsistent merchandising, poor service, and frequent out-of-stock conditions. Brennan's command-and-control attitude, conveyed by a hard line and disagreeable edicts, did not motivate employees to change. Not only that, but he did not do anything to correct the perception among his management team or employees that change was a bad thing. He never told his employees what was changing and why.

control change. The flyer showed that a regular human being would be leading the seminar, but I was not surprised. I really did not expect that I would be attending a seminar led by God. What was disappointing was that this flyer claimed this human being knew how to manage change.

The traditional assumption that change can be managed is not only false, but also contradictory. Managing implies control, and in today's dynamic environment, people cannot control change. Change can be good or bad— but if you try to manage change or resist it, you are history. Seventy percent of all organizational change fails not because the change was bad, but because the method for introducing it was badly orchestrated and, therefore, created resistance. Tolerating change is not enough, and managing change is not possible. The power of change must be harnessed to create the agility needed to compete in today's dynamic marketplace.

The Science of Change

The fast and discontinuous nature of change is a science that must be understood. The science of change begins with the relationship between change and pain. Pain often accompanies change; this is perfectly natural. On a personal level, pain is a body's signal that it is being harmed or is harming itself. In business, it is a sign that an organization is harming itself. This pain may be felt in quality problems, competitiveness, customer satisfaction, turnover, and so on. The challenge, then, is the resilience of the organization in responding to pain. How does the organization absorb and respond to change?

If the speed of change is less than an organization's resilience, then the organization can harness the energy of change, respond to it with agility, and succeed. If the speed of change is greater, then the pain of change will be too much. So, since no organization can control the speed of change, it is critical that the organization build up its resilience and the ability to manage its resilience capacity.

Resilience

Resilience is the ability to bounce. If you hold a ball at shoulder height and drop it, and the ball bounces back up to your shoulder, a mechanical engineer would say that it has a resilience of one. If the ball does not bounce at all, then it has a resilience of zero. If it could bounce back twice as high, then it would have a resilience of two.

People have resilience, too. It is our ability to absorb change, and it can be measured in points. For example, if I have 1,000 personal resilience points, I might decide to allocate 700 points to my work, profession, and company while 200 points go to my family, 50 to my church, and 50 points to country and community. If my business is doing well, and it is growing with more work than capacity, I may actually be using 850 resilience points rather than 700. Meanwhile, at home, I have a wife who wants me to slow down, two daughters who work for my company, and a son in college. All of my family is very active and we spend a lot of time together. So, it appears that I am using 350 resilience points on my family rather than the 200 I allocated.

What does this mean? It means that if I come in to work and my administrative assistant says, "Jim, that meeting you have planned for 9:30 has been changed to 10:00 because one of the principals who is supposed to call in cannot get to a phone until that time," I hit the roof. I say, "What do you mean, it's 10:00? Don't they know the schedule? I can't be changing things around like this! I've got work to do. I've got to make this happen in a timely manner!" Then I look at myself and say, "What an idiot. I am a complete dipstick. What a jerk."

What makes me like that? After all, the change in meeting time probably requires about one-tenth of a resilience point. It barely registers. However, if I have no points left, then a tenth of a point is more than I can give.

The science of change involves careful consideration of these resilience points. It is based on building resilience capacity, both personal and organizational. If I am successful in building my resilience capacity, then I can then apply it to someone else's resilience capacity. Before long, I can build the organization's resilience capacity so that it can harness the energy of change at the current rate of change.

The three guidelines for building personal resilience capacity are:

1. Raising resilience capacity comes both from increased pain management and remedy management.
2. Lowering the effort needed to harness the energy of change requires a person to deal with the perceived levels of certainty and control.
3. The agility to deal with change comes from having a balanced life.

Raising organizational resilience capacity to harness the energy of change is based on four factors:

1. Organizations must increase their understanding of the positive effects of change and the negative effects of not changing.
2. Organizations must increase certainty and control.
3. Organizations must be assured that their personnel are in alignment with their focus for the future.
4. Organizations must become agile so that they can respond to change.

An organization that considers these factors when building resilience capacity also understands what I call the four "Boomerang Principles."

Here is the first principle: What comes back will be exactly the same. When you throw a boomerang, the same boomerang returns. An organization that harnesses the energy of change will mirror the feelings, thoughts, and commitment put forth by its leaders.

The second principle is: What comes back will always be more than what was put forth. Imagine if a boomerang could gain momentum and return at a faster speed. In an organization that harnesses the energy of change, the synergy that evolves acts as a multiplier for the evolution of renewal progress, improvement, growth, and success.

The third principle is this: Results are never obtained until an investment is made. A boomerang will not return if it is not thrown. How long it takes to return depends on various complex factors and is difficult to predict. It will return, however, and an organization that has harnessed the energy of change recognizes that fact.

The fourth principle is: Benefits will be positive only if the organization's leaders know how to throw the boomerang. It takes practice to know how to throw a boomerang. For an organization to harness the energy of change, the leader must know how to nurture the process, overcome difficulties, and emphasize business agility. With effective, insightful leadership, an organization will find No Boundaries between its strategic vision and making it a reality.

Organizations That Understand Change

An organization that understands change has a number of identifying characteristics. For one, each employee has clearly defined responsibilities, accountabilities, roles, and identities. However, at the same time, not one of those employees is ever heard saying, "That's not part of my job description." That's because the organization does not shackle its staff to outmoded ways of thinking to which they can cling when change occurs. Instead, the expectations of each employee are delineated and are altered after conference and mutual agreement.

Another characteristic is continuity in the organization's purpose without inflexibility. Organizational focus is actively, not reactively, maintained. These organizations may re-conceptualize missions and goals, but they still keep their vision in sight. Also, the focus of employees within the organization is consistent with the organization's focus. However, everyone in the organization understands the necessity of change. All employees believe that change will benefit them both personally and professionally.

An organization that understands change practices effective communication, since communication is vital to the health of an agile company that harnesses the energy of change. Businesses are often full of secrets. Their executives do not believe that employees need to know the strategic plans and paths of the organization. You will not see that in an organization that understands change. In those organizations, employees are encouraged to participate in and provide feedback to organizational changes. Information flows through the organization in a timely manner.

An organization that understands change is ready to apply this understanding to harnessing its energy to create an agile supply chain. Only with understanding can the organization strive to meet the seven requirements necessary for harnessing the energy of change.

Harnessing the Energy of Change

Harnessing the energy of change involves meeting seven requirements. These requirements are flexibility, modularity, upgradability, adaptability, selective operability, automation supportability, and nimbleness. The goal is to create the agility that allows companies and supply chains to anticipate customer needs and expectations and produce accordingly. The result is a foundation upon which an understanding of Supply Chain Excellence may be based. The sections that follow discuss these requirements.

Flexibility and Modularity

Flexibility and modularity are the first two requirements necessary for harnessing the energy of change to achieve Supply Chain Excellence. Build-to-order (BTO) manufacturing has grown tremendously. It seems everyone is jumping on the BTO bandwagon, from PC makers, to automakers, to seismic-enclosure makers. No longer does it make sense to build to stock and then configure the order. Instead, companies are receiving the order and then building, and the only way to keep up with the demand is through flexibility and modularity.

Although flexibility and modularity are both necessary in the total integration and BTO environments, there is a difference between the two. Flexibility means being able to handle a variety of requirements without being altered. Flexible manufacturing systems, therefore, are those able to produce a variety of different products without altering the manufacturing operation. These systems must be "soft" and "friendly" rather than "hard" and "rigid" because they must be able to address the change in variety and handle products that vary in size and features.

Whereas flexibility deals with variety, modularity deals with volume. Modular manufacturing operations are those that can produce more or less of a product without changing the method. Products made to order must be made quickly when the orders are received, so systems must cooperate efficiently over a wide range of operating rates. Manufacturing has changed and will continue to change. With flexible and modular manufacturing processes, supply chain partners can address the changes. It is by having this flexibility and modularity that organizations gain the agility to synthesize supply with demand.

Upgradability

The changing manufacturing environment, from "if we build it, they will come" to "they have come, so we must build," also demands that systems and processes be upgradable.

Upgradability is the ability, with a minimum amount of downtime, to gracefully incorporate advances in equipment, systems, and technology. All sorts of products, from computer drives to battery re-chargers to DC converters are now featuring upgradability. With the accelerated rate of change, it is no longer economical to replace entire systems as we have in the past. Instead, the system should be able to move to the next level without stumbling or hiccupping and with little downtime.

Adaptability

Adaptability provides a setting for flexibility, modularity, and upgradability. We may have a beautiful strategic master plan and think we know everything will work. Everything seems perfect and on-target. But what happens if a portion goes wrong or an external factor changes?

An adaptable environment allows us to take sudden changes in stride. Traditionally, emphasis has been placed on controlling operations to conform to system requirements at a "steady-state" level. Steady state no longer exists— and averages are irrelevant. Systems now must be adaptable to respond to changing system requirements.

Adaptability takes into consideration the implications of schedules, calendars, cycles, and peaks. It allows a system to work well at 9:15 a.m. on a Tuesday in the summer slow season and at 2:30 p.m. on a Friday during peak demand times. The design, from

The Value of Flexibility and Modularity — GE Lighting

To maximize manufacturing flexibility and quality at its Hendersonville, NC, plant GE Lighting turned to a conveyor-fed assembly system. Management at the plant decided that a flexible system built around workstations coupled with a computer-controlled system with agility was the best solution for its operations approach. The plant managers also made a $2.2 million investment in equipment that included a complete overhaul of materials handling operations and manufacturing processes on the 800,000-square-foot shop floor. For example, conveyors and work carts feed work-in-process to workstations. An automated data collection system provides real-time analysis and performance reports. In addition, lift trucks that operate in the plant have been outfitted with wireless laptops, eliminating a paper-based system that was untimely and inaccurate. The end result is a $1.6 million annualized saving in plant costs. — *Modern Materials Handling*, April 1, 2002 an operations perspective, must allow it to work for a one-hour time frame, a two-hour time frame, or a two-week time frame. Adaptability also recognizes that product demand in various industries is higher at some times than others and can adjust accordingly. If you build adaptability into your plans, processes, and systems, you will rarely be caught by surprise.

Selective Operability

The ability to operate selectively is key to a successful supply chain. Therefore, supply chain elements must be able to operate in segments, allowing for implementation one segment at a time without degradation of the overall system. An understanding of how each segment operates is also required. Then, if something goes wrong, we can answer questions such as, "How did this take place? What has this done to our level of customer satisfaction?"

Selective operability also allows us to put contingency plans in place. A company that locates its distribution center on the North Carolina coast must plan for hurricanes so that other sites are not affected when a power outage, flooding, or roof damage occurs. If the company has a site in Wisconsin, it must be prepared for blizzards so that they do not affect production in a West Coast manufacturing plant. This can be tricky because operating in segments tempts a focus on individual links, but in reality, this approach continues to view the chain as a whole. It is only by looking at the flow from start to finish that you can make contingency plans so that the flow does not come to a grinding halt in the middle.

Automation Supportability

As time has marched on, factories have become more and more automated. Supply chain elements that are not automated now soon will be. Implementation will be piecemeal, and non-automated elements must support this type of implementation. Therefore, it is imperative that all elements throughout the synthesized supply chain not only support neighboring elements, but also integrate and interface with them. Integration is necessary for two automated processes, and interfacing is necessary for one process that is automated and one that is not.

Nimbleness

During slowing or slow economic times, it is difficult to escape the gloomy portraits painted by analysts, politicians and business journalists. For example, in 2000, *The Wall*

Street Journal declared, "Making things is out of fashion," adding that everyone "seems to be ditching factories." Now, in the wake of the World Trade Center and Pentagon tragedies that added to an already sluggish U.S. economy, industry reports are even more negative. Their implication is that manufacturing is declining. In actuality, it is production that is declining, and that's because inability to respond to and harness the forces of change has caused individual companies to fail. We live in turbulent times that demand a new set of rules. Direct-to-consumer delivery channels, customer satisfaction, customization, shorter cycle and lead-times, smaller lot sizes, and build-to-order have effectively and irrevocably rendered "business as usual" obsolete. To survive in the new economy, companies and their supply chains must rely on nimbleness.

Being a nimble enterprise does not mean using nimble manufacturing practices. A nimble enterprise is a company that responds as opportunities present themselves. In other words, a nimble enterprise is ready to change direction or reinvent itself as the business climate changes. Its emphasis is on organizational readiness rather than specific products or markets. For example, a nimble enterprise might recognize that automobile manufacturing has moved offshore permanently because there are real cost savings in that practice. However, that same enterprise might also recognize that appliances cannot be manufactured offshore and imported economically and set its sights on manufacturing appliances. Or in response to new FAA security procedures, a luggage manufacturer may choose to design new carry-on pieces that allow passengers to carry more things in less space and all in one bag, rather than figuratively wringing its hands because fewer people are flying and luggage does not sell like it once did.

Why Agility Is a Core Competency of Supply Chain Excellence

Agility should be the result of applying the seven concepts discussed above. Agility should not be confused with nimbleness. Nimbleness is still based on reactions, whereas agility is stronger and involves being active. Consider a kitten and an adult cat. A kitten will pounce if something moves in front of its face; it is nimble. A cat will look for moving objects and then pounce; it is agile.

In the business world, agility is a combination of predictive and preventive actions that arises from harnessing the energy of change. The difference can be discerned when a convenience store is used as an example. A nimble convenience store tracks its customers' purchases, studies the information, and makes sure it stocks the products needed to satisfy the needs of all customers. An agile convenience store not only tracks what its customers are purchasing, but also when they purchase it and what kind of customers they are. It uses this information to change displays and cashiers throughout the day to appeal to the customers that regularly frequent the store at a certain time and purchase certain things.

I can tell you, by looking at a photograph of a customer and a cashier, what time of day it is in the convenience store without any other information. Early in the morning, before 7:00 a.m., the customers are contractors and subcontractors grabbing coffee and a biscuit or sweet roll before they head off to a work site. From 7:00 a.m. to 9:00 a.m., the customers are businesspeople looking for cappuccino and a bagel to consume on their drive into the office. At noon, the customers are the subcontractors and contractors looking for sandwiches and chocolate milk. At 5:00 p.m., the businesswomen and businessmen return to purchase items for a quick meal before evening activities with the kids get started.

If it were my convenience store, I would staff the store with cashiers that appeal to all the customers, designing their shifts around the times that those particular customers are stopping in. I would change displays during the business lulls to put out the products the next wave of customers is most likely to want so that they can get them quickly and easily. For my dinner crowd, I would negotiate with a fast food chain or local deli to provide products for busy families on the go. This is what being agile means and, as you can see, it is more than just stocking what your customers buy.

Agility requires a new set of rules. These are:

- Using the right mix of old employees, new talent, and technology to generate creative tension, disturb the status quo, and propel the company forward
- Establishing direct links with customers to listen to their needs, complaints, opinions, and suggestions
- Creating alliances between IT (those who create and morph technology) and the salespeople (those who communicate with customers on a regular basis)
- Emphasizing that change is constant and should neither be feared nor resisted, but embraced
- Establishing new measures of success
- Embracing continuous improvement as a prerequisite for success
- Studying marketing and customer data to establish trends and anticipate needs

By following these new rules, a company and its suppliers can work together in the supply chain to manufacture quality products, get them delivered to the right place on time, satisfy customers, increase return on assets, and reduce costs.

Changes in the fundamental structure of businesses create substantial changes in the ways employees work within that business. Some of these changes are direct and can be handled quickly. Others are indirect and tend to affect an organization's strategy and competitive advantage. They can reduce market share, alter the distribution network, and cause the company to rethink customer needs.

For example, an environmental testing firm sold its products domestically for many years. The manufacturing staff, therefore, only wired and calibrated equipment for the U.S. market. During a lull in the domestic market, the firm decided to sell its product internationally.

The sales team then made its biggest sale ever: an Australian firm bought entire lines of its product. Unfortunately, this sale, which had so much potential, fell flat. Why? Because no one told the manufacturing staff that Australia's electricity runs on 220 volts, not 110 volts. The manufactured goods did not work in Australia: they had been manufactured for a 110-volt market. Somewhere along the pipeline, someone forgot to relay key information.

As the above story also demonstrates, the supply chain is not in a steady state. By expanding the reach of its product, the company needed a different supply chain, but instead they relied on the one they had always used. In other words, a great supply chain today may be terrible six weeks from now. We live in a dynamic world, and only those who achieve Supply Chain Excellence can respond. The pursuit of Supply Chain Excellence is also a process of continuous improvement that embraces and harnesses change to create the agility necessary to satisfy the ultimate customer. Agility permanently rekindles individual creativity and responsibility and creates a transformation of a company's internal and external relationships—relationships with No Boundaries. That is why agility is one of the core competencies necessary for achieving Supply Chain Excellence.

8

Peak-to-Peak Performance

"Once you are labeled 'the best' you want to stay up there, and you can't do it by loafing around. If I don't keep changing, I'm history."
— Larry Bird

To many people, success is the ultimate goal, and they would be hard-pressed to associate success with failure. Yet, peak performance is often the beginning of failure. As radio commentator Walter Winchell once observed, "Nothing recedes like success." How can this be? Doesn't success breed success? That's what we've all been told. Also, we were all told at one time that the Pilgrims were the first English-speaking settlers of America. Neither is true.

Winston Churchill said, "Success is rarely final." Benjamin Franklin said, "Success has ruined many a man." Now, they were on the right track!

The natural order of life is peak-to-valley-to-peak-to-valley, and so on. This is like a basketball team that exhausts itself chipping away at a large point deficit and consequently lacks the momentum to pull out the victory. The peak represents success and the valley that follows, failure. This can be explained by a quote from Henry Kissinger, who said, "Every success only buys an admission ticket to a more difficult problem."

Analogous to this statement is the American education system. A student starts at a lower level and works him or herself up to the next level, and then the process starts all over again. A student begins in the lower grade of middle school, for example, and as he or she learns and succeeds in that grade, he or she is promoted. Success! In the last year of middle school, the student is on the top of the peak. Success at that level promotes the student out of middle school and into high school, and then what happens? The student is back at the bottom of the valley again, and he or she has to climb back to the top. Success is measured by a diploma, which sends the student either out into the world for that first job, or on to college—either of which puts the student back on the bottom, and the climb begins again.

You can circumvent this process with Peak-to-Peak Performance. In fact, if you don't work toward achieving Peak-to-Peak Performance, success will ruin you and take down your supply chain. You will follow success with failure. This chapter addresses Peak-to-Peak Performance, refutes the myths of consistency and success, and explains why Peak-to-Peak Performance is necessary for achieving Supply Chain Excellence.

Peak-to-Peak Performance

As the founder, president, and CEO of a supply chain consulting firm, I have taken my organization from success to failure, from failure to success, and from success to success. Through my experiences, I have determined there are four evolutions of a company:

1. Fail/fail
2. Fail/succeed
3. Succeed/fail
4. Succeed/succeed

Fail/fail is usually a vicious cycle that keeps destroying confidence until the ultimate failure occurs: The company stops trying. The top leaders of these companies cannot afford to have the patience of Thomas Edison, who believed each unsuccessful result brought him a step closer to success, or Abraham Lincoln, who failed repeatedly in business and politics before rising to save our nation. The nature of business is more realistic.

What puts companies in a fail/fail cycle? They do not learn from their mistakes. As the saying goes, "Insanity is doing the same thing over and over and expecting different results." There are many companies like this. You do not hear much about them because they never succeed. Often, these companies are led by CEOs who will not admit they make mistakes and who run around blaming others in the company for their failures. Such companies enter the fail/fail cycle quickly.

Fail/succeed is when your mistakes teach you how to overcome setbacks. A good example is the retail giant that, after suffering failure, hired a new CEO who looked at his predecessor's failures, saw the good in them, recognized the bad, and began working with his management teams to eliminate the bad. Currently, the retail chain is a dominant player in its market. Those who view failure as a challenge can turn adversity into the motivation to succeed.

Succeed/fail is the most common progression for people and organizations. Consider the "sophomore jinx," which can turn a sensational freshman or rookie into an average player during the second season. In the entertainment field, most movie sequels fail to match the excellence of the originals, and in literature, an author's second book may not measure up the first. Examples of companies that have experienced succeed/fail are numerous. You see their "going out of business" signs every day or read in the newspaper that they've filed for bankruptcy, or you hear that they are being sold. In the case of many start-up dot-coms, their Web sites have vanished from cyberspace. I can name examples from almost every industry: automotive, retail, publishing, printing, pharmaceutical and healthcare, and so forth.

Succeed/succeed is the final step in this evolution. An organization that learns the formula to succeed/succeed is like the basketball team that knows how to take the lead and add to it, with strong defense and daring offense. They play to win instead of playing to avoid losing. The key is continuous improvement. A company that practices continuous improvement will remain in the succeed/succeed cycle and will, therefore, achieve Peak-to-Peak Performance.

Peak-to-Peak Performance involves the continuous process of beginning anew and climbing to a new peak, and then the next peak, and the peak after that. It means that a company should not wait for outside factors to force its hand, but instead should innovate on its own terms and prepare for challenges before they arise, while being wary of the naysayers. The process that helps a company move from peak-to-peak is called Revolution, which makes sense when you consider that Peak-to-Peak Performance requires innovation and preparing for challenges before they arise. These are the characteristics of most good revolutionaries. Such succeed/succeed revolutionaries include John Wooden, former coach of the most successful college basketball team of the 20th century, UCLA, who said, "It's what you learn after you know it all that counts." Another is the late Jerry Garcia, leader of the Grateful Dead, the most successful live rock band of all time. "You don't just want to be considered one of the best," Garcia said. "You want to be considered the only one who does what you do."

Success Can Be Hazardous

Success can be hazardous to an organization's health because most organizations cycle through the fail/succeed and succeed/fail modes. They begin with a surge of entrepre-

Succeed/Succeed — Intel

Intel has enjoyed huge success and profit from its microprocessors, the most well-known of which is the Pentium. However, in 1995, as Intel saw the life cycle of its products decreasing from eight years for the 386 series to a much shorter period, the company decided to examine the sales-order computer system it was using. The system tracked pricing, orders, delivery, and inventory. Orders from the United States, Japan, Asia, and Europe were handled on separate systems and then rolled together so that they could be tracked on the domestic system. This setup was unable to keep track of inventory and was not Y2K-compliant.

Intel decided to replace the system with enterprise resource planning (ERP) software and managed to install it during a time when Intel's annual revenues were increasing from $18 billion to $26 billion and its employee roster was growing from 40,000 to 60,000 employees. After the new system was installed, the company was able to track inventory all over the world, commit it to a customer, and deliver it in three days.

Two years later, Intel decided to halt growing shipping costs before they reached $1 billion (which was the forecast for 2001). It reshuffled its global logistics and directed a major portion of its production flow to three new warehouses located next to airports in Malaysia, the Philippines, and Costa Rica. These facilities are integrated, handling both parts and materials that arrive from suppliers and other Intel plants, and outbound/finished chips slated to be delivered to customers. Intel now can guarantee its air-freight contractors full or almost-full airplanes, which results in lower freight rates. Intel also redesigned its packaging to nest twice as many cartridges safely in each carton. This saves $1 million per week in shipping costs.

Intel rode the success of this system during the boom years of the Internet, but in 2000, the company again started to slump, mainly because of a downturn in personal computer sales caused by the recession. Undaunted, the chipmaker switched gears and began work on a new form of chip: 0.13-micron processors on 300mm diameter wafers; the first processors were released in February 2002. Microprocessors produced on 300mm wafers cost 30 percent less than those made using 200m wafers, and combining the larger wafers with its advanced 0.13-micron process let Intel quadruple the output per wafer. In addition to packing more chips onto a larger diameter wafer, 300mm manufacturing will use 40 percent less energy and water than a 200mm wafer factory, according to Intel. By May 2002, Business Week was reporting that Intel had "nailed" the transition to a 0.13-micron process that is accelerating the introductions or faster chips while also reducing costs.

Why did Intel do all this? So that it would continue to succeed instead of failing. It uses continuous improvement regularly to make sure that it moves peak-to-peak. So far, it is working.

neurial energy and climb the mountain to success, achieving peak performance. They become smug, even arrogant, stop being entrepreneurial, protect their success, decline, land fail. Their performance falls and they find themselves in a valley. Like the retailer I mentioned earlier, they bring in new leadership, reorganize, refresh the entrepreneurial spirit, and once again climb the mountain to success. Once they have reached this peak, the cycle begins again. In fact, this cycle will generally continue over time until an organization loses touch with its own mortality and cycles from succeed/fail into a fail/fail. Then everyone asks, "What happened? How could such a great company go out of business?"

Another hazard of success is the consistency myth. Many people and organizations believe that since consistency often takes them to the peak, it will keep them there. This is just not so. Although consistency is necessary when producing a quality product, it does not necessarily allow the agility needed to adjust to changes. It can often drag a company down to the valley. As Aldous Huxley once said, "Consistency is contrary to nature, contrary to life. The only completely consistent people are the dead." The same is true of organizations. If they are completely consistent, they will be dead.

Business has always been difficult, and it has become even more so, with the globalization of economics and the speed of the Internet. In these changing times, a business has two choices. It can cycle through the succeed/fail routine, which, with its barrage of downsizing, rightsizing, restructuring, repositioning, and reengineering, is the dominant pattern of business today. Or the business may choose to revolutionize the fundamental way it does business and strive to become better than the best, to grow, and to be successful today, tomorrow, and into the future. It all starts with the realization that today's peak performance is tomorrow's good performance, next week's average performance, and next month's poor performance. It also means realizing that consistency must be pursued sometimes and abandoned at others, depending on a particular situation. Consistency that is bound to the quality of a product and consistency in meeting work schedules should be pursued, but consistency is not always the answer in other aspects of business.

The Principles of Revolution

To achieve Supply Chain Excellence, organizations must apply the principles of Revolution to the supply chain. Consider the prerequisites for the Revolution that leads to Peak-to-Peak Performance:

- Commitment to continuous improvement
- Harnessing the energy of change

Motivational Leadership — Ralph Larsen of Johnson & Johnson

For healthcare giant Johnson & Johnson, 2001 was the 69th consecutive year of sales increases and the 17th straight year of double-digit earnings-per-share growth. Johnson & Johnson's stock was up 14 percent for the year. The company was also launching drug-coated coronary artery stents, which could generate anywhere from $500 million to $3 billion in sales in 2003, according to analysts.

Former CEO Ralph Larsen was the force behind these figures and the company's latest successes, which include being ranked in the top 10 of Fortune's Most-Admired Companies. In 1997, Larson rallied 900 top managers around the theme of innovation. "We thought we were paying a lot of attention to R&D, but our scientists didn't think so," Larsen recalls. Fired up by the rally, the company made some savvy acquisitions, put a scientist on its executive committee, and successfully leveraged its name into the faster-growing and more profitable drug and medical-device sectors. — *Fortune*, March 4, 2002

- Motivational leadership
- Revolutionizing the culture
- Alignment

Do you recognize any of these? You should, because the first two were covered in other chapters. Let's discuss the other three.

Motivational Leadership

Although leadership is not a set of traits, true leaders have the following characteristics:

- Integrity—the leader lives and tells the truth
- Credibility—the leader is accountable, genuine, and open
- Enthusiasm—the leader shows excitement about the future
- Optimism—the leader focuses on success
- Urgency—the leader knows that the only way to impact the future is to act today
- Determination—the leader steps forward to face doubts and uncertainties, to accept risk, to move forward, and to make real his or her understanding that there are No Boundaries between his or her organization and competitive advantage. Leaders act.

Relying on these characteristics, leaders motivate others by the way they communicate with, work with, and treat others. Leaders recognize the importance of effective communication, and they arm people with the certainty and control that allows them to harness the energy of change through direct communication and the sharing of information. When leaders make decisions, they adhere to the "three rights": the right decisions at the right time communicated to the right people. They enjoy their work. Finally, leaders treat others in the way others want to be treated.

Motivational leaders create the environment necessary for achieving Supply Chain Excellence. They seek out other motivational leaders in their supply chain partnerships and share skills and knowledge. They also recognize that instantaneous dissemination of information with No Boundaries among partners is critical to achieving Supply Chain Excellence.

Revolutionizing the Culture

Culture is the personality of an organization, but it is also the personality of a supply chain. Any Revolution that tries to change merely the inanimate portions of the supply chain—facilities, equipment, transportation—will fail unless it changes the people involved and how they interact with one another. Revolutionizing a culture is no simple task, for an organization's culture will try to stifle the introduction of a new one. Cultural Revolution also must go beyond simple changes in the cultural manifestations and perceptions. It must transform the organization's culture. It must transform the rules, habits, procedures, standards, norms, rewards, language, jargon, stories, expectations, ceremonies, and titles that affect cultural conformance, organizational behavior, and organizational performance.

The foundation for this transformation is a shared, consistent vision of where the organization is headed. Everyone must be aligned with a commitment to dynamic consistency, the underlying basis of which is "improve, improve, improve." This means understanding the difference between "change, change, change," and "improve, improve, improve."

Revolutionizing the culture in the supply chain involves more than one organization. Often several corporate cultures are involved. But if the different cultures can align themselves to the vision of continuously improving the ultimate customer's satisfaction, then they can achieve Supply Chain Excellence.

Alignment

An organization achieves alignment when it can accomplish the following:

• Connect its employees' behavior to the company's mission, turning intentions into actions

- Link teams and processes to the changing needs of customers
- Shape business strategy with real-time information from customers
- Create a culture in which these elements all work together seamlessly.

The same principles apply to an extra-organizational collaboration among supply chain partners. The seamless connection between the producer of raw materials and the ultimate customer is the essence of the supply chain.

Why Peak-to-Peak Performance Is a Core Competency of Supply Chain Excellence

When supply chain partners commit themselves to Supply Chain Excellence, they also commit themselves to continuous improvement, agility (by harnessing the energy of change), motivational leadership, revolutionizing their cultures, and alignment. They understand that continuous renewal is not a program that ends, but rather an ongoing process. They accept that they are the underdogs because they are on top. And finally, they will experience the non-stop evolution with No Boundaries to higher levels of Peak-to-Peak Performance.

Peak-to-Peak Performance is critical to the success of the supply chain and that is why it is a core competency of Supply Chain Excellence. At the same time, Supply Chain Excellence is also critical to the success of Peak-to-Performance in the increasingly globalized, build-to-order, electronic marketplace.

9

Supply Chain Holism

"To a hammer, everything looks like a nail."
— Mark Twain

The following are examples of problems companies face today:

- Company A has a SKU explosion that has created a shortage of warehouse space.
- Company B has a manufacturing capacity problem on a new, hot-selling item.
- Company C has a customer satisfaction problem.

Now, consider these questions. Should Company A's problem be solved by manufacturing smaller lot sizes or should it be solved by adding square footage to the warehouse? Should the solution for Company B's problem be adding capacity to manufacturing or increasing yield or increasing uptime? Should the resolution of Company C's problem be reconfiguring the distribution network or installing a new warehouse management system or implementing a continuous improvement process?

What are your answers? How did you think these problems should be solved? You may find that your solution has less to do with the problem than it does with your area of expertise. One expert might view these problems as warehouse-related. Another expert might argue that they are systems problems. Yet another expert might declare that they are maintenance problems. The reality, however, is that to identify and solve these problems, these experts must work with others who have complementary skill sets. The companies must assure the experts practice Supply Chain Holism, a solution with No Boundaries. This chapter defines Supply Chain Holism and explains why Supply Chain Holism is a core competency of Supply Chain Excellence.

External Collaboration — Sears and Michelin

Early in 2001, Sears and Michelin wished to improve supply chain practices that would lead to increased sales and reduced costs. After completing an audit of both companies' internal systems and processes, they identified a list of actions required to optimize the supply chain. These included:

- Establishing a single, shared data source and focusing efforts on product availability
- Enhancing the ability to collaborate through increased information visibility
- Reducing the possibility of surprises that are costly to the supply chain (i.e., lost sales, excess inventory, premium logistics expense)
- Leveraging future demand information to reduce inventory levels while maintaining fill rates
- Improving the understanding of each company's business process and identifying gaps that could be eliminated through process changes and information flow
- Gaining the ability to generate and direct "alerts" to decision-makers so that issues could be resolved prior to addressing customer service

The two companies then implemented a collaboration process that is fully supported by senior management at both companies. Sears and Michelin can view supply chain metrics using a single shared data source, thus allowing adjustments to be made. As a result, inventory at Sears distribution centers has been reduced by 9.5 percent, and Michelin has initiated programs to positively impact its inventory levels while maintaining high fill rates. In addition, business rules are now set that trigger exceptions to which decision-makers at each company must respond on a weekly basis. This activity has become part of an efficient business process that is proactive to avert stock-outs. The new capability and its available metrics are being used for Sears/Michelin monthly sales, inventory, and marketing meetings. — *Supply Chain Alert,* June 16, 2002

What Is Supply Chain Holism?

Supply Chain Holism is the integration of the warehouse, logistics, manufacturing, quality, maintenance, organizational excellence, and systems. It is a concept that stretches from the planning of a site through the determination of the correct network to the cultural ties that bind employees to an organization's mission. It is the expression of Link Excellence, which is Level 2 of Supply Chain Excellence. Link Excellence involves all the link's elements working as one for ongoing, incremental improvements, as well as innovation, communication, and leadership.

The same concept expressed beyond the link is Collaboration, Level 4, which consists of judicious partnerships with suppliers, vendors, customers, contract manufacturers, and anyone else along the supply chain. You cannot achieve Supply Chain Excellence without both Link Excellence and Collaboration.

By looking at the whole link, Supply Chain Holism assures an organization

- The correct distribution network
- The correct manufacturing methods
- The correct warehousing methods
- The correct operating systems
- The correct maintenance methods
- The quality to satisfy customers
- The correct process for continuous improvement

As you can see, Supply Chain Holism does not focus on one technology or component. That would be like trying to build a house with only a hammer. Building a house takes more than a hammer: It takes a saw, a ruler, a paintbrush, a screwdriver, and a variety of other tools. So, too, does building an excellent link in the supply chain: Many parts are involved, and no one piece is more important than another. Supply Chain Holism recognizes this.

Supply Chain Holism and Logistics

Supply Chain Holism is based on understanding that logistics cannot be managed apart from all other operations in a company. Logistics must be integrated with everything else to bring harmony to the supply chain because—despite old understandings—supply chains are not simply about logistics. They are not simply about distribution. Instead, they are about everything: inbound and outbound transportation, material handling, preventive and predictive maintenance, statistical process control, manufacturing methods, customer satisfaction, inventory management, production planning, partnerships, teams, information, warehousing methods—in short, the entire operation.

The first time Tompkins practiced Supply Chain Holism was more than ten years ago. A major appliance manufacturer had hired us. We removed inventory, streamlined procedures, and improved customer satisfaction. Everything was functioning like clockwork until a fancy German machine that made the appliance shell went down for two weeks. The fallout was almost catastrophic. New homeowners were unable move into their houses because they did not have appliances and, without them, could not acquire certificates of occupancy. Dealers were unhappy because there were no products. Eleven days later, the machine was fixed, but the damage had been done.

The president of the company said to me, "Jim, we need to put all of the inventory back in. We will never, ever do that again."

I replied, "Sir, I agree with you. You should never, ever do that again. But you cannot put the inventory back in."

His face got red, and he stood up. "Jim," he said, "What am I going to do without the inventory?"

I said, "You never, ever, ever let that machine go down again. If you can't make sure 100 percent that that's true, then you build a second one and let it sit there looking at the first one, because you can buy ten of those machines cheaper than you can put that inventory and that glut back in the system."

He said, "You're hired."

I said, "Thank you. What's the assignment?"

He answered, "Do maintenance on that machine."

I went back to my company and asked, "Does anyone know how to do maintenance? I don't know how to do it! What are we going to do?" Of course, I really knew what I had to do. I hired someone to do maintenance.

Supply Chain Holism—and, thus, Supply Chain Excellence—are impossible without understanding maintenance—and quality, manufacturing, logistics, warehousing, organizational excellence, and systems. There must be a pursuit of excellence in all functional areas, not simply logistics.

To achieve true Supply Chain Excellence, holism must be spread across the breadth of the supply chain. Again, there should be No Boundaries. If this is not done well, the result will be a never-ending list of unmet commitments that will impact the entire supply chain. This lack of performance will ultimately create poor customer satisfaction and result in the loss of market share for all the supply chain's links. Therefore, it is critical that holism be pursued across all supply chain links and not simply within each link.

Why Supply Chain Holism Is a Core Competency of Supply Chain Excellence

Pursuing Supply Chain Holism demands that

- The distribution network for the supply chain be designed from the perspective of the entire supply chain and not from the perspective of any one link
- The proper manufacturing and warehousing methods be performed in the context of the whole supply chain
- The ultimate customer quality expectations be understood by all links and be the driving force for defining maintenance and quality requirements throughout the supply chain
- All links understand the continuous improvement efforts of other links so that the continuous improvement process is focused on the chain and not the links
- The people throughout the supply chain be aligned and committed to the process of Supply Chain Excellence

Designing the distribution network across the entire supply chain may be achieved through distribution synthesis, which will be addressed more fully in Chapter 12. Basically, distribution synthesis is making sure that the right manufacturing operations and right distribution centers are in the right locations holding the right amount of inventory, and that the right transportation is being used to satisfy the customer. Done from a link's perspective, this is called logistics. When it is done from a chain's perspective, it is called Supply Chain Holism. It is the harmony that evolves throughout the supply chain by adopting Supply Chain Holism that results in true Supply Chain Excellence.

Manufacturing is no longer a peripheral player in the success of the supply chain. Performing manufacturing and warehousing across the entire supply chain involves manufacturing synthesis, the subject of Chapter 11. Briefly, manufacturing synthesis involves small lot sizes, short lead-times, short setup times, and responsive manufacturing—all to be responsive to the needs of the supply chain. It includes warehousing and manufacturing practices driven by the correct systems—Warehouse Management Systems (WMSs), Manufacturing Execution Systems (MESs), Enterprise Asset Management (EAM), and Advanced Planning and Scheduling Systems (APSs).

The correct WMSs (those required by Supply Chain Holism) are real-time, bar-code-based, radio-frequency (RF)-based systems that maximize warehouse performance. The correct MES provides critical information on manufacturing decision-making and enables product engineering to improve on product design through historical repair-work tracking.

The correct EAM treats asset management as an integrated process, not just automation of a set of administrative tasks. The correct APS is a robust package that provides multi-site control over the manufacturing process, thus strengthening responsiveness and reliability. These systems and others are addressed more fully in Chapter 15.

What do these systems have in common? For one, all of them are necessary for manufacturing synthesis. They also rely on integration and they also do not operate in a vacuum. The truly effective examples integrate and interface with each other, creating an intelligent warehouse where computer systems, material handling equipment, storage equipment, and people form a single, cohesive unit. Supply Chain Holism sees and understands that the boundaries between manufacturing and warehousing are blurring and will one day be eliminated.

The third requirement—understanding customer expectations—is part of the Supply Chain Holism focus on the ultimate customer. It demands an awareness of the customer up and down the supply chain, as well as an awareness of the customer's definition of quality. Proper maintenance and quality methods and procedures must be in place to protect against breakdown and/or defective products, and there must be no buffer that allows interruptions in service to disturb the links in the supply chain. Serving the customer is the foundation of this focus, but what is even more vital is the customer's satisfaction.

The fourth requirement for Supply Chain Holism is that all links be aware of other links' continuous improvement efforts, both inside the organization and out. It prevents the sacrifice of one link for the optimization of another and eliminates statements like, "The left hand doesn't know what the right hand is doing." For example, when a major mouthwash manufacturer and a major retailer worked as a chain and not as independent links, sales of the mouthwash increased $8.5 million. The companies shared information throughout the chain to increase on-shelf availability, and this combination of Visibility and Collaboration netted increased sales. This success laid the foundation for an even more aggressive process of continuous improvement.

Supply Chain Holism views all operational functions as a unit. If one part of that unit is improved, then the rest must be also. So, Supply Chain Holism emphasizes continuous process improvement—supporting Supply Chain Excellence does.

The fifth Supply Chain Holism requirement involves people and attitude. People are what truly enable excellence, and their attitudes, more than any other single factor, drive the success of Supply Chain Holism. If everyone involved in Supply Chain Holism is committed to the goal of satisfying the ultimate customer, everyone wins.

High Employee Satisfaction and Superior Performance — Clarke American Checks, Inc.

Headquartered in San Antonio, Texas, Clarke American supplies personalized checks, checking account and bill-paying accessories, financial forms, and other related services to more than 4,000 U.S. financial institutions. Clarke American believes that empowered and accomplishment-oriented associates are its greatest competitive advantage, and it fully recognizes the correlation between high employee satisfaction and superior performance.

The company's culture and values are focused on putting the customer first, integrity and mutual respect, knowledge sharing, measurement, having a quality workplace, recognition, responsiveness, and teamwork. Its employees regularly apply standardized quality tools, performance measurement, technology, team disciplines, and specialized skills as part of their job functions. Work teams and improvement teams carry out efforts to attain operational improvements based on clear, direct business goals, while cross-functional project teams promote "change the business" initiatives. Systematic approaches to communication and a highly competitive team excellence award process facilitate shared knowledge across the teams.

Individual initiative and innovation are expected. Associates are encouraged to contribute improvement ideas under Clarke American's Suggestions, Teams, Actions, Results (STAR) program. In 2001, more than 20,000 process improvement ideas saved the company an estimated $10 million. Implementation rates for STAR ideas increased from less than 20 percent when the program started in 1995 to 70 percent in 2001. At the same time, financial rewards flowed back to associates, who averaged nearly $5,000 in bonus and profit-sharing payouts.
— *Baldrige Award Recipient Profile,* March 12, 2002

Perhaps you have noticed a pattern here. If you have, then you are on the right track. The pattern is, simply, that Supply Chain Holism and Supply Chain Excellence share similar goals with an ultimate destination—total integration. Both look at the whole through shared information and processes, and so both add value to the whole.

10

Supply Chain Excellence and Customer Satisfaction

"Customers only pay for what is of use to them and gives them value."
— Peter Drucker

The power in the marketplace has shifted from producers to consumers. At one time, customers would hear, "You want that car in red by Friday? I'm sorry, but that's not possible. You can either purchase it in green here today or you can wait six weeks for another shipment of red cars to come in." Now they hear, "You want a blue shirt on Monday for $15? Absolutely. No problem. How else can I help?" Increasingly, end-users are dictating the pace of change. For example, in the last two years, customer demands have altered the look of the basic recliner chair. "Consumers of today are much more savvy about design and demanding about what they want," says Kerry Shannon, design coordinator for Eggert Furniture.

Reebok, responding to consumer demand for classic pro basketball attire, has brought back its Legacy basketball shoe, which was popular in the late 1980s. It is clear that today, the synchronization of supply with demand is critical to achieve customer satisfaction.

Customer satisfaction is critical to Supply Chain Excellence and competitive advantage. Therefore, Supply Chain Excellence emphasizes creating and maintaining close, good relationships with customers. When customers' thoughts, wants, and needs drive innovation and flow of goods and services from raw materials suppliers to retailers and ultimately back to those customers, you have customer satisfaction.

Customer satisfaction is not customer service. Customer service measures how well a company performs against internally generated standards called key performance indicators (KPIs). For example, a few years ago, I was sent out of my way to the wrong gate by a major airline that claimed it had been ranked first in customer service each year from 1994 to 1997. I was informed by a ticket agent, "We usually do use this gate for Cincinnati, but not today. There is no way you can make it to gate C-32 in time." I was very unhappy. I was a customer of that airline and I was not at all satisfied. That's because that airline is not really interested in its customers or their satisfaction. What they are interested in is meeting and exceeding their measure of customer service, which is on-time arrivals. Their method for meeting this measure is to pad their schedules so that, even with a high level of incompetence, they can appear to be on time. This is what I like to call "Customer Service Self-Centeredness," and it has nothing to do with satisfying the customer.

This chapter explains the difference between customer service and customer satisfaction, defines customer satisfaction, and explains why customer satisfaction is a core competency of Supply Chain Excellence.

Customer Satisfaction Is Not Customer Service

There is often a major disconnect between internally measured customer service performance and actual customer satisfaction. Manufacturers measure their performance of KPIs —order-fill rates, on-time shipments, and order-picking accuracy are common ones. KPIs are important, but meeting them does not necessarily mean that customers are being satisfied. Customers base their satisfaction on how easy it is to conduct business—the quality of information available, consistency of receipt timing, and so on.

I'll use one of our clients as an example. One of our principals told me, when I asked how the client he was working for was doing on customer satisfaction, "Great." "Super," I replied. "How do you know that?"

He answered, "Here's their chart on fill rate, here's their chart on backorders, here's their chart on on-time deliveries, here's their chart on damage, and here's their chart on complaints." Every one of these charts was impressive. I then asked him if he had spoken with any of our client's customers. He said no, so we called several. Here is what we heard:

- "If there were anyone else that could fill the orders for the products we need, we'd go to them."
- "This company is not reliable."
- "We place one order but receive three shipments. These folks are clowns."
- "These people aren't doing good work."

- "I can't read their invoices. I don't have a clue what I'm supposed to be paying on this paperwork they send me."
- "I call their customer service and they put me on hold for an hour and a half and then make me talk to some stupid computer."

Another client had a similar story. The president told me the history of his firm and its many years of success. Then, he told me that the last two years of his company's history were years of stagnation, losses, and personal anguish. I began probing. After covering several topics, I finally asked, "How are you doing with customer satisfaction?"

He responded, "I can't explain why our customers are so unhappy with us; we are doing a super job on customer service."

I did some research and discovered the following:

- Customer service was defined as orders being shipped, as ordered, two days after receipt, with an order fill rate above 90 percent.
- The company was shipping the orders accurately 99.2 percent of the time, doing it within two days 99.4 percent of the time, and achieving an order fill rate of 99.7 percent (by lines).
- Customer complaints were infrequent.
- Although customer service was good, there was a feeling that customers were not happy.

The Value of Customer Satisfaction — Roche Laboratories

Roche Laboratories Inc., is the marketing and sales subsidiary of pharmaceutical company Hoffmann-LaRoche Inc. Roche has a "Keep Customers First" strategy that drives its systems implementation. Recently, Roche implemented a new, state-of-the-art e-business order-management system. Roche's goal was unparalleled satisfaction levels and the assurance that its business partners share in the advantages of lowered transaction and information costs.

Now, over 85 percent of Roche's purchase orders are received via e-business, with a target of 90 percent or more. Also, Roche receives payment data electronically for over $1 billion per year in electronic payments. The result? Improved customer satisfaction. They've shortened turnaround times, which is always important, and maintained order consistency. — Customer Case Study, Sterling Commerce, 2002

This feeling was caused by the fact that repeat orders were, for an unidentified reason, down.

The situation with both of these clients was Customer Service Self-Centeredness. Customer Service Self-Centeredness can destroy companies slowly or quickly. It can only be cured by a shift in thinking away from customer service and toward customer satisfaction.

What Is Customer Satisfaction?

Customer satisfaction is the measure of a supply chain's effectiveness. It is the means by which companies in a supply chain attempt to differentiate their products, keep customers loyal, improve profits, and become the supplier of choice. In other words, it is an ongoing, escalating, process of adding value, meeting requirements, and exceeding expectations.

Customer satisfaction is a scientific process. Its formula was discussed in Chapter 2. It requires companies to divest themselves of their self-interests while fixating on the needs, expectations, and perceptions of those to whom they provide products and services. Supply chains must know and be able to identify the special needs of each level of their customer base. This means understanding the customer tiers and using data mining to create a data chain that allows supply chains to identify the needs of each tier.

The Customer Tiers

No company or supply chain has only one kind of customer. A customer base is made of people, and no two are alike. Each person has his or her own set of expectations, and each requires different services. Identifying the many different aspects of a company's customer base is vital. Such identification can be as broad and thorough as a company chooses, as long as one critical point drives it: Every customer is different and demands different levels of service.

For example, one of our clients, a grocery chain, and I were discussing customers. I asked, "Who are the customers, really?"

The reply was, "We've got lots of customers."

"But where do you make your money?" I persisted.

The client didn't know, so a market research firm was hired to do a study. When the study was complete, the research showed that the grocery chain had three kinds of customers: those who spent $20 a week in the store, those who spent about $75 a week, and those who spent $150 a week. Those who spent $20 a week cost the client $3 each time they visited the store; those who spent $75 a week earned the client $6 each time they visited the store; and those who spent $150 a week earned the client $30 each visit. In this case, then, three levels of service were necessary. Unfortunately, the client did not understand that the customer level that brought in the most money should receive the best services. Instead, the chain created a special cashier for the customers spending only $20 a week while their best customers waited in longer lines.

People also change while they are an organization's or company's customers; therefore, companies cannot maintain customer satisfaction with the same set of services and value-adds that satisfied yesterday. As customers progress in their patronage, they will expect more and require more to be satisfied. Customer satisfaction, as a core competency of Supply Chain Excellence, is a continuous improvement process. It is not a policy to implement; it is a process to be pursued continually.

Understanding the basic customer tiers enables companies to pursue customer satisfaction in a highly focused and specialized manner. The tiers are three levels of customers with three corresponding levels of satisfaction. The first is the visitor level. Visitors are customers who occasionally purchase products and services but have no lasting commitment to the company. To them, satisfaction comes from the fundamental aspects of the product. These customers define satisfaction in terms of product features and cost.

The second level is the *associate* level. Associates are customers who regularly, but not exclusively, purchase a company's products and services. Because the associates' experiences have grown since they started out as visitors, their expectations have also increased. As they become associates, they begin to take features and cost for granted and turn their attention to quality. This is a serious challenge because different customers define quality differently.

The third level is the *partner* level. Partners are customers who have moved a company to the primary position on their lists in a product category. Through time and maintained satisfaction, they have come to the place where they always choose their preferred company first. Like associates, however, their expectations have grown and so have their requirements for satisfaction. They still expect features, cost, and quality, but they also require new value-added support like special handling, special delivery, extra services, training, and so on.

To maintain satisfaction while transforming visitors into partners, companies must know their customers well enough to evolve with them. They must keep in mind that customer satisfaction grows out of focusing on the ultimate consumer and that all customers must become partners if the companies are to achieve Supply Chain Excellence. This will win continuous customer satisfaction.

How Customer Satisfaction and the Customer Tiers Work Together

Consider a situation in which a company produces an excellent product at a competitive cost with high quality, but little extra value added. Let's say the company delivers service that each customer perceives as being valued at 100 points. If that customer is a visitor, whose expectation of service is only 40, then their customer satisfaction is high at a 60 (100 − 40 = 60). However, if that customer is an associate, who expects an excellent product, competitive cost, and high quality and therefore had a point value of 90, then their customer service is low at only 10 (100 − 90 = 10). If that customer is a partner, who expects an excellent product, competitive cost, high quality, and considerable value-added support and has a 110-point expectation of service, then the level of customer satisfaction is negative 10 (100 − 110 = −10). This can be described as a customer dissatisfaction level of 10.

These examples explain why the president of the company with the long history was having difficulty. As customers' expectations increase from visitor to associate to partner without a corresponding increase in the customers' perception of service received, satisfaction quickly becomes dissatisfaction. The company thought that customer satisfaction would remain the same if the company kept the same level of service or improved it slightly. The firm did not try to keep pace with its customers' increased expectations. This eventually will position a company for failure.

Mining Data and the Data Chain

Once you have familiarized yourself with the customer tiers, you will want to work on taking your customers to the partner level. Various methods and technologies exist for identifying overall customer needs, including software that tracks overall buying patterns. To take your customers to the third tier, it is important to do data mining within an enterprise data warehouse to create a data chain that not only allows you to be proactive with your customers but also contributes to your supply chain's agility.

Data mining is a set of statistical techniques used to identify the trends, patterns, and relationships in data. Analysts use some of these techniques to examine data, while other techniques are somewhat automated and can recognize patterns. Most data mining tools can create several different mathematical models from data, but two models are especially popular. They are classification and clustering. Classification techniques assign the data to classes determined by an analyst. Clustering techniques identify occurrences in the database with similar characteristics and then group them into clusters.

Data mining can also be used to analyze customer acquisition and retention promotions over time, to learn which combinations of products are purchased, and to identify meaningful market segments using profile and Web activity data. For example, an analyst might assume that people buying wireless phones will buy the replaceable batteries the phone manufacturer recommends, but what if customers are actually buying less-expensive batteries designed for a different product? In this case, a data mining analysis could point out an opportunity to promote the value of using the recommended batteries over the cheaper batteries.

Data mining has gotten a lot of hype recently, and those who write about it make it seem like a simple solution. In actuality, like all technology, data mining must be used wisely. Also, while data mining tools are automated and often Web-based, it still takes people who understand data and statistics to use the results of data mining to take customers to the partner level. This can be accomplished by:

- Making sure the data is well prepared and using as much detailed data as you can.
- Selecting the right tools through understanding the potential users, the structure of your data, and the likely job requirements.
- Using the knowledge that you and those experts who understand data and statistics have of the business to point the tools at the right data.
- Letting those experts explain and redirect efforts.

The result of using data mining correctly are is a data chain—a combination of customer data used to anticipate customer need and provide the appropriate products. Customers then enjoy the benefits of knowing that their preferences and needs are being considered, and they retain a favorable impression of the provider. This leads to increased revenues and, more importantly, increased customer retention and loyalty. As these customers keep coming back and providing feedback that allows new product designs or current product improvements, they become partners.

The Requirements of Customer Satisfaction

Customer satisfaction has specific requirements that must be met. These requirements are grouped in three categories: pre-transaction, transaction, and post-transaction. In the pre-transaction category, these requirements are

- Availability information
- Quality sales representation

- Stock level information
- New product and package development information
- Target delivery dates scheduled and communicated
- Regular reviews of product depth and breadth

The transaction requirements are

- Ordering convenience
- Order acknowledgement
- Credit terms
- Handling of questions
- Reliable order cycle times
- On-time and frequent deliveries
- Order status information and tracking capabilities
- Fill rate and back order percentages
- Product substitutions
- Emergency order filling capabilities

Post-transaction elements are

- Invoice accuracy
- Returns and adjustments
- Well-stacked loads
- Easy-to-read and quality packaging

If your chain meets these requirements, then you are on the path to Customer Satisfaction. For example, a 2002 *IndustryWeek.com* survey of manufacturers with more than 1,000 employees revealed that 55 percent of companies with customer retention rates of more than 80 percent are using customer satisfaction requirements of real-time customer order-tracking, and that group is also using real-time customer order data to reserve inventory (44 percent) and capacity (26 percent). Overall, 58 percent of the companies responding to the survey are differentiating products and services based on customer classification.

These companies are on the right track. They are allowing the customer to be the co-creator of value, and they promote ongoing customer dialogue. They also indicate that these companies believe that it is good business to treat customers as individuals rather than as demographics.

Why Customer Satisfaction Is a Core Competency of Supply Chain Excellence

Consider the questions that must be answered to bring about high levels of customer satisfaction. They are:

- Who is the customer?
- What does the customer want?
- How do we increase customer satisfaction?

Companies frequently define and identify all sorts of customers, knowing that they must exceed their wants, needs, and expectations. Supply Chain Excellence requires that the entire supply chain—and not simply one company—ask these questions. All links must focus on the ultimate customer until the entire chain is aligned with the ultimate customer, or the end-user. This alignment, by its very nature, increases customer satisfaction. This is because everyone along the supply chain has adopted a culture for customer satisfaction based on a shared, consistent direction for the entire supply chain and an attitude of progressive, open, continuous improvement and learning.

Now, consider a few of the specific steps for increasing customer satisfaction. They are

- Reducing costs
- Increasing quality
- Promoting teamwork
- Responding to customer needs
- Creating the customer data chain

If you take these steps, which are generally applied to a company, and apply them to the supply chain, you can achieve Supply Chain Excellence. Simplifying the processes of manufacturing and distribution, reducing scrap and rework, and eliminating operations and delays, which are the output of Supply Chain Excellence, all reduce costs. Encouraging employees of every organization along the supply chain to go beyond "doing it right the first time" to "doing it better the next time," also an element of Supply Chain Excellence, increases quality. They establish standards and implement process control at all levels to achieve these standards and allow the shipment of orders accurately without stockouts.

When a supply chain achieves Supply Chain Excellence, everyone along the supply chain communicates the information necessary for gaining competitive advantage for that

Meeting Customer Needs — Theory of Postponement

Traditionally, manufacturing did all the work, and warehouses simply stored the product. Blurring the boundaries between manufacturing and warehousing until there are No Boundaries is what Supply Chain Excellence is all about. By getting the value-added activities closer to the customer (i.e., doing them at the warehouse at the last moment before shipment), organizations can eliminate double handling of product, increase customer responsiveness, and add more value to SKUs throughout the pipeline. This is postponement, and there are two types.

One simply delays the customization of product. An apparel manufacturer might produce the same dress for seven different distributors. Through cooperation of the supply chain partners, the warehouses receive the one dress, generic thus far, and place labels and tags on it to meet the specific requirements of the customers. The manufacturer can concentrate on making the apparel and not tie up resources performing operations that the warehouses can do later on in the pipeline.

The second type of postponement is called merge-in-transit. This is a process used frequently in the computer industry. Components are received in the warehouse from various OEMs and CEMs: a keyboard from A, a CPU shell from B, a mouse from C, a hard drive from D, and so forth. Kitting and packing occurs at the warehouse based on customer specifications.

With postponement, manufacturers have less inventory to control, warehouses take an important role in the supply chain (rather than being perceived as a cost center, which is traditional), and customers receive what they want. Postponement operates with No Boundaries.

supply chain, and that promotes teamwork and creates synchronization and agility. After all, we are in a world that defines competition as supply chain vs. supply chain rather than company vs. company. Through Supply Chain Excellence, the supply chain responds to customer needs because cycle times are reduced, flexibility is increased, and customers in trouble receive the assistance they need. In summary, Supply Chain Excellence and customer satisfaction are irrevocably intertwined. You cannot have Supply Chain Excellence without customer satisfaction and that is why it is a core competency of Supply Chain Excellence.

11

Manufacturing Synthesis

"A great factory with the machinery all working and revolving with absolute and rhythmic regularity and with the men all driven by one impulse, and moving in unison as though a constituent part of the mighty machine, is one of the most inspiring examples of directed force that the world knows."

— Thomas Nelson Page

uppose your circulatory system was not connected to your gastrointestinal system and both systems worked quite well apart from each other. At first, this might seem to be a satisfactory arrangement. Your blood flows well and you are digesting your food with few ill effects. However, what would you do if you wanted toxins removed from your blood by your kidneys? You would have to connect the systems and hope for no leaks.

Poor connectivity between biological systems is the equivalent of boundaries between functions on the supply chain. These boundaries require manual connections, which, in turn, may cause leaks. In other words, the connections create problems that would not arise if the functions worked as an organic, agile, and synchronized whole with No Boundaries. This is particularly true for manufacturing, which functions much more efficiently and effectively when its processes are synthesized.

Now, imagine that someone comes along and tells you that your circulatory system is not necessary at all and you should remove it. How long do you think you would live? Interestingly, that's what SCM says about manufacturing. SCM often treats manufacturing as a peripheral player in the success of the supply chain, when in actuality, without manufacturing, there would be no integration, no synthesis, and no Supply Chain Excellence.

As SKU customization and customer-ready product preparation are postponed to the last possible minute, traditional roles in manufacturing are becoming less of a means for securing competitive advantage. To remove the boundaries from manufacturing and merge these traditional roles, manufacturing synthesis is necessary.

Manufacturing synthesis is the combination of lean manufacturing, agile manufacturing, cellular manufacturing, and the 12 Requirements of Success for the Future Capable Company. This chapter defines lean, agile, and cellular manufacturing, introduces the 12 Requirements of Success for the Future Capable Company, explains manufacturing synthesis, and demonstrates why manufacturing synthesis is necessary for Supply Chain Excellence.

Lean Manufacturing

Mass manufacturing cannot provide the increased capacity, increased throughput, faster cycle times, lower WIP inventory, reduced setup time, and smaller lot sizes that manufacturers need to be agile-the key to survival in today's global, customer-centric marketplace. Mass manufacturing is geared for the "if we build it, they will come" mentality. Today's customers are not that accepting. They demand quality and customized products delivered to their doors almost as quickly as they can click on a link or place a phone order. Lean manufacturing provides the agility, velocity, efficiency, and quality needed to satisfy today's savvy customers.

Some powerful industry players have been touting their lean manufacturing processes for a number of years, including John Deere, Cessna Aircraft, Cisco Systems, Magna Donnelly, Boeing, Johnson Controls, Freudenberg-NOK, Raytheon, Korry Electronics, and the Timken Company. However, as IT and e-tail boom, lean manufacturing is no longer regarded as just an interesting method of production fit only for certain manufacturers. Today, companies from a pork pie producer in England to a seal manufacturer in Kalamazoo, Michigan, are all using lean manufacturing.

Lean manufacturing, which is based on the Toyota Production System, is a series of flexible processes that allow the manufacture of products at lower cost. "Lean" is used to describe it because, when compared with mass production, it uses less of everything. It eliminates non-value-added waste in the production stream, and its theoretical objective is a lot size of one. A lean manufacturer is continuously improving in the direction of this theoretical objective.

The elements of lean manufacturing include:

- Equipment reliability—Equipment that runs when needed.
- Process capability—Processes that always produce quality.
- Continuous flow—The material flows in small lots through production.
- Error proofing—Ways to prevent the product from being built incorrectly.
- Stop-the-line quality system—If items of poor quality are appearing on the production line, the line is stopped.
- Kanban system—A material flow system that pulls materials through the production process based on customer demand.
- Visual management—When utilized fully, a new employee can understand how to do a job from the visual information in the plant and all employees understand the performance of the plant.
- In-station process control—Each workstation has the information and equipment for the worker to inspect and produce good quality parts.
- Quick changeover—A system to change from one product to another quickly.
- Takt Time—Production is paced to customer demand. Takt Time equals the time available to produce a product divided by the number of parts that the customer wants to buy.

These elements all help eliminate waste, and cutting waste is the foundation of lean manufacturing. Waste is defined as "anything that consumes material or labor without adding value to the end product that is received or purchased by the end customer."

Implementation of lean manufacturing is often referred to as de-massification and can create the following results:

- Reduced inventory
- Increased productivity
- Reduction in the floor space required to make a product
- Reduced scrap and rework
- Reduced lead-time
- Reduced changeover time

Agile manufacturing is one step beyond lean manufacturing. Agile manufacturing was developed as a response to a number of issues:

- Fast and unpredictable turbulence in the marketplace
- The demand for high quality, low volume, and short product life cycles
- The decline of mass production

The Value of Lean Manufacturing — Mitsubishi

In 1998, Richard Gilligan, formerly a manager at Ford, became chief operating officer of Mitsubishi Motor Manufacturing of America Inc. His job was to turn around a 10-year-old plant with more than 3,100 employees where quality had become an issue. In 1999, one of every four cars in the plant needed some type of repair work.

Gilligan began the turnaround by making changes that included making quality assurance the responsibility of line workers rather than quality inspectors. He also reduced the number of managers from 13 to six and began informing employees how well the plant was doing statistically via newsletters and meetings.

In addition to working with employees, Gilligan increased the number of standardized parts that could be shared among various vehicle types. He helped establish a commonality of the types of parts that go unnoticed by the consumer. For instance, door handles used on all the different vehicles are the same.

The plant produced 193,435 vehicles in 2001. In 2000 it had its highest year ever of 222,036. Interestingly, the plant has also reduced its reliance on automation after it was determined that robots attaching the plastic bumper covers to the front of the car were not performing efficiently. So the plant replaced the robots with humans. The plant's assembly line was also redesigned. In some areas in the plant, the vehicles would pass above worker heads as they moved to other lines. Workers found they could continue working on those vehicles if they were brought down to the floor.

Lean manufacturing has increased efficiency, production, and sales at that plant. In January 2003, the plant will be able to handle the manufacture of Mitsubishi's new sports utility vehicle. — Auto.com, June 14, 2002

- Customer satisfaction
- Demands for high levels of value-added services
- Products that are rich in information
- A focus on people and relationships

The characteristics of agile manufacturing include

- Customer enrichment
- Competitiveness through cooperation
- Organizational focus on change and uncertainty
- A highly educated and empowered workforce

- Emphasis on the customer as an individual
- Relationship-driven partnerships
- Flexible management structures
- Virtual corporations
- Products and services rich in information
- Integration and flexibility

Agile manufacturing has four underlying principles: delivering value to the customer, being ready for change, valuing human knowledge and skills, and forming virtual partnerships. Two critical elements of agile manufacturing are flexibility and modularity. To review what was discussed in Chapter 7, flexibility means a variety of items can be manufactured with little or no change in procedure or methodology. Modularity means that manufacturing is capable of producing different volumes of items with little or no change in procedure or methodology.

The Value of Customer Modularity — Bayer Diagnostics

Bayer Diagnostics' ADVIA is the first multi-functional sampling workstation that does not require blood-test batching. Until ADVIA was offered, managing anemic patients meant using two machines for two different blood tests, which was staff- and setup-intensive. ADVIA provides hospitals and clinics more versatility, as well as more efficiency in their phlebotomy operations. Daily maintenance is automated, less space is necessary, cross-training employees is easier, and one entire workstation has been eliminated.

Cellular Manufacturing

Cellular manufacturing helps companies reduce WIP and respond to change more quickly, both of which are goals of manufacturing synthesis. In cellular manufacturing, Group Technology principles are used to design efficient cells. Each cell is focused on producing "families" of parts. Process sequences maximize the layout, resulting in smaller batch quantities that run through the cell with little material handling and small WIP inventories. In other words, the parts continually flow through the cell in process sequence, from start to finish, without ever leaving the cell. Typically, companies considering cellular manufacturing produce a wide variety of complex but similar parts.

The Future Capable Company

A Future Capable Company responds to the forces of change while using the proper application of technology. It not only focuses on the best solutions for today's requirements, but it also focuses on the solution after the next solution and moves from peak to peak to peak. Its role is that of a "change insurgent," emphasizing organizational readiness rather than specific products or markets. Therefore, it is an organization that searches technologies for business applications, or "killer apps," and looks at other organizations with a view to capturing newly emerging technologies and markets at the speed of light. It is also flexible and adaptable, ready to suddenly change direction and utilizing lean, agile, and cellular manufacturing principles to accomplish such change. It sources services and supplies through the Web, gives suppliers equity, and relies on performance-based pay, stock options, project teams, and contract workers.

By its very nature, a Future Capable Company follows a specific set of rules that includes:

- Using the right mix of old employees, new talent, and technology to generate creative tension, disturb the status quo, and propel the company forward
- Establishing direct links with customers to listen to their needs, complaints, opinions, and suggestions
- Creating alliances between IT (those who create and morph technology) and salespeople (those who communicate with customers on a regular basis)
- Emphasizing that change is constant and should neither be feared nor resisted, but embraced
- Establishing new measures of success
- Embracing continuous improvement as a prerequisite for success.

By following these new rules, the Future Capable Company accepts and understands that boundaries and channels are blurring. Manufacturing cannot remain competitive in the global marketplace if it is contained in a large factory that owns raw materials plants, manufactures parts from those raw materials, assembles them, creates buffer stock from the assemblies, and ships them to the warehouse. Nor can it exist in a vacuum as one link not fully synthesized in the supply chain. Today's factory may very well be virtual, with manufacturing functionalities existing in every link in the supply chain. Suppliers, manufacturers, and customers must cooperate and collaborate to survive in the war of supply chain vs. supply chain by achieving Supply Chain Excellence.

The Future Capable Company embodies a philosophy of dynamic consistency and complies with these two critical qualities:

1. It is a continuous process of "improve, improve, improve."
2. It is anchored on a full, integrated understanding of 12 Requirements of Success

It has three distinct tasks: understanding the 12 Requirements of Success, understanding external issues, and understanding internal issues. Since these are of critical importance to Supply Chain Excellence, I'll describe them briefly here. My book, *Future Capable Company: What Manufacturing Leaders Need to Do Today to Succeed Tomorrow,* covers them in more depth.

The 12 Requirements of Success for the Future Capable Company are:

1. **Cost**—This means scrutinizing transportation, acquisition, distribution, inventory, reverse logistics, packaging, and manufacturing and examining the supply chain for ways to significantly reduce costs and increase profitability. Cost reduction within the plant is of value only if those lower costs are passed along the entire supply chain.
2. **Customer Satisfaction**—This means meeting customer requirements and exceeding customer expectations through customization that uses value-added activities.
3. **Global**—Success depends heavily on an integrated global strategy. This means reaching out to other countries and pushing aside boundaries to promulgate goods and services. If you are not everywhere, you are nowhere.
4. **Speed**—As John Chambers of Cisco Systems says, "It's not the big that beat the small, but the fast that beat the slow." This means being quick to respond to customer needs and relying on principles like BTO to deliver just as quickly.
5. **Certainty/Change**—When activities conform to well-established and clear standards, errors, disruptions, and crises are rare. However, change must be expected, harnessed, and responded to smoothly.
6. **Control**—This calls for a straightforward and transparent inventory control system, efficient material flow, and up-to-date and upgradable material tracking and control while simplifying all processes.
7. **Balance**—Balanced manufacturing and supply chain operations result in drastic inventory reductions. Large inventories are a liability.
8. **Quality**—Quality is conformance to customer requirements and calls for a continuous quality improvement process.

9. **Maintenance**—Maintenance is much more than just the care of physical assets used in a production operation. Instead, it combines reliability, predictive maintenance, and preventive maintenance to create high levels of uptime and productivity, anticipate potential problems, and minimize future problems.

10. **Human Capital**—Organizations must value intellectual capital and secure its growth by making sure all employees are satisfied, happy, and challenged; otherwise continuous improvement is not possible.

11. **Continuous Improvement**—What is a great process today will be suspect in a few months and obsolete shortly thereafter. Therefore, it is imperative that manufacturers continually evaluate, analyze, and improve processes.

12. **Synthesis**—The Future Capable Company must synthesize all functions and ensure that decisions are made in the context of the supply chain and the needs of the ultimate customer.

The 12 Requirements of Success for the Future Capable Company are the foundation for manufacturing synthesis, which also requires understanding external and internal issues.

Understanding external issues demands an awareness of factors outside a company that affect it. These factors include shifts in the marketplace, availability of new technology, actions taken by competitors, and government regulations. If a company does not stay aware of external factors, it will become self-centered and lose touch with reality. Once this happens, organizations have difficulty establishing priorities. They may begin doing the wrong things.

Understanding internal issues requires awareness of a company's business plan. Manufacturing management should be intimately involved in the business planning for a company. The priorities for manufacturing should be established within the context of the company's business plan. The most important priority is manufacturing synthesis.

Manufacturing Synthesis

Manufacturing synthesis combines lean, agile, and cellular manufacturing to reduce lead-times. Long lead-times make it impossible to plan and control priorities. Long lead-times make it impossible to respond to the synchronization of supply with demand. Shorter lead-times clear the shop floor of WIP inventory, conflicting manufacturing priorities, and other manufacturing problems. Manufacturing synthesis can be summarized in two words: continuous flow. Continuous flow means balancing a series of operations for reduced production lot sizes to create a continuous, controlled indexing of parts through production. Continuous flow, with its short lead-times, provides for the agility manufacturing needs to synchronize supply with demand.

Manufacturing synthesis can be accomplished by

1. Reducing lead-times significantly
2. Reducing production lot sizes and setup times
3. Minimizing all uncertainty and increasing discipline
4. Balancing all manufacturing operations
5. Implementing a straightforward and transparent production and inventory control system
6. Reducing inventories drastically.

The sections that follow discuss these elements more fully.

Customer Lead-Times

There are three types of lead-times: manufacturing lead-time, production lead-time, and customer lead-time. Manufacturing lead-time is that period that begins when material becomes available at the first manufacturing operation and ends when the last manufacturing operation is complete. Production lead-time is the period from the ordering of all materials for items in production until the last manufacturing operation is complete. Customer lead-time is the period between the time the customer orders and the time the customer gets what he ordered. Manufacturing synthesis requires significant reduction of customer lead-times. This depends on the historical approach to lead-time and the amount of product customization. The less attention that has been focused on lead-time before, the greater the opportunity.

To reduce customer lead-times significantly, the methodology for doing business must change. The procedures to be followed are as follows:

1. Document present customer lead-time. Hard data is necessary if a company is truly dedicated to reducing customer lead-times. Record times for each activity in a flow chart that accurately documents actual occurrences, not standard operating procedures.
2. Conduct a competitive analysis. This research should be global. The more a company can learn about what its partners and competitors are doing and how lead-times differ

The Value of Manufacturing Synthesis — John Deere

The John Deere Commercial Products plant in Grovetown, Georgia, manufactures complex utility tractors that require 3,500 assembly steps. However, using advanced flow manufacturing techniques, the plant's well-trained, self-directed workforce can finish the job in under four hours with the help of automatic guided vehicles (AGVs) with onboard computers.

The AGVs operate in a fully integrated and networked assembly system called a "smart device network." They are precisely routed through assembly steps along a "racetrack" to cross-trained operators using smart tools at workstations. This is a radical departure from traditional powered assembly line handling techniques. The AGVs are more flexible and cost-effective. Downtime for repair and maintenance is less.

To compensate for seasonal swings in product demand, assembly workers are flexed up and down the line and even between Grovetown and a second tractor facility in Augusta, Georgia. When off the line, they might be involved with additional training, special projects, or various continuous improvement projects or even visiting suppliers with supply chain problems.

In addition, all workers are cross-trained at their home workstation as well as the workstation immediately ahead of and behind them on the line. This has several advantages. Productivity gains of up to 25 percent are possible, and operators can help others if they fall behind. Also, the plant attitude shifts from "not my job" to team spirit.

Inventory flow improvements have been occurring since the system went live. Workers use wireless terminals with built-in bar code scanners to receive inventory from suppliers and to manage the flow of inventory from storage to the line. The information is fed directly to the enterprise resource planning (ERP) system. From there, it is sent on to suppliers for replenishment, and when the manufacturing execution system (MES) is completed, to touch screens at the workstations, keeping operators up to date in real time on inventory availability.

To upgrade and expand the plant so all this could happen, Deere invested in the 62-vehicle AGV system and acquired smart assembly tools, 106 new workstations, and an additional 188,000 square feet of space. Fifty vehicles circulate around the main assembly line loop (the racetrack), which is 1,452 feet long. Two spur or feeder lines are used for engine and transmission assembly. Six AGVs work the engine line. Six more are on the transmission line. Deere operations managers follow the progress of work-in-process (WIP) on computer monitors. Payback is expected to be less than three years. — *Modern Materials Handling*, April 1, 2002 globally, the better prepared it will be when it sets its lead-time reduction goal. Comparing data, creating charts, and conducting gap analyses are all excellent methods for analysis.

3. Establish a goal. The organization's leadership should initiate and guide the establishment of lead-time reduction goals. These goals should include a commitment to reducing customer lead-times by analyzing the flow chart that documents present customer lead-time and rethinking the methods of doing business. This can be accomplished by recording the goals for each activity on the flow chart. The total of goals for each activity should surpass the reduction required to achieve the overall goals.

4. Identify bottlenecks. Bottlenecks are the constraints that lengthen the time of an activity and create longer lead-times. Customer lead-time should be used in the identification process. Many activities on the chart could have bottlenecks. Once they are identified, a series of customer lead-time reduction teams should be chartered to eliminate bottlenecks and reduce lead-times.

5. Create multi-department teams. These teams should be broad-based and comprised of individuals who focus on specific sets of activities. They should have the authority to change business methods to achieve the lead-time goals. They should also emphasize simplification, embrace teamwork, and eliminate uncertainty.

Short customer lead-times make it possible to plan and control priorities; thus, reducing customer lead-times will create lower inventories, quicken customer response, improve employee satisfaction, improve quality, and reduce manufacturing costs. Customers will benefit from receiving their orders quickly, and that increases market share. Employees will be more satisfied because they will be working for a responsive, successful company. Even quality will improve.

Production Lot Sizes

Reducing production lot sizes, which is facilitated by reducing setup times, shortens manufacturing lead-times. You can reduce production lot sizes as follows:

1. Document present lot sizes.
2. Identify specific lot sizes for reduction.
3. Reduce setup times by following the Toyota Motor Company concepts and techniques (see below).
4. Calculate the economic lot size (where setup cost equals the inventory carrying cost).

5. Identify alternative methods for handling the economic lot size between operations.
6. Evaluate alternative methods for efficient material handling.
7. Justify the investment required to reduce setup times and to handle materials efficiently, with the savings resulting from the reduction in lot size.
8. Define and obtain support for specific improvement plants.
9. Implement the reduced setup time and the material handling equipment as justified and begin production of reduced lot sizes.

The concepts developed by the Toyota Motor Company to reduce setup are:

1. Separate the internal setup (setup activities that must occur inside a machine and require that it not be operating) from the external setup (setup activities that occur apart from the machine and can take place while the machine is in operation). Assure that all external setup operations are complete before the machine is taken out of production. Only internal setup activities should be performed when the machine is out of operation.
2. Convert as much of the internal setup as possible to external setup. By altering the machine or the setup activities, the total setup time can be minimized.
3. Eliminate the adjustment process. By altering the machines or the setup, a standard or automatic setting can be established that eliminates the need for adjustment.
4. Abolish the setup. Standardizing parts can lead to an elimination of setup. Another approach is to have parallel operations performing different operations and, by switching a mechanism, using only the operations that apply to each product.

To apply these concepts, you should standardize the external setup actions and the machines, use quick fasteners, use a supplementary tool, consider multi-person setup crews, and automate the setup process. Reducing setup times makes a reality of high-variety, high-productivity, low-inventory, and small-lot-size manufacturing. This is manufacturing synthesis.

Uncertainty

Minimizing uncertainty must begin with a definition of events that have caused surprises, crises, or changes in plans. First, survey a cross section of manufacturing personnel to obtain an initial list of target events. Follow with an ongoing activity in which manufacturing personnel record events that result in surprises, crises, or changes in plan.

Minimizing uncertainty also means creating standards and establishing discipline. A standard of performance must be established, accepted, and followed. Everyone involved must understand and respond to the following standards:

- Product quality
- Delivery schedule
- Delivery quantity
- Process performance
- Process duration
- Machine downtime
- Setup duration
- Production methodology
- Part tolerances
- Product packaging.

Discipline is the resolution to embrace a standard and not accept anything other than performance at or above the standard. This discipline must be uncompromising and applied uniformly throughout a company. There can be no exceptions. All vendors, organizational elements, and production operations must have this level of discipline.

Minimizing uncertainty will bring quiet, order, and stability to manufacturing so that harmony and continuity will exist in an error-free, disruption-free, crisis-free environment. Events that impair manufacturing, such as sloppy product development schedules, quality problems, maintenance problems, unreliable employees, and untimely vendor shipments, are no longer part of the manufacturing process. This allows the continuous flow that is so critical to manufacturing synthesis.

Balance

Balanced manufacturing operations require continuous flow (already defined), focused departments, sequential flow, and standardization. Having focused departments means that all operations required to produce a family of parts are in a focused area. "Sequential flow" means the unchanged flow of parts through a series of operations. Standardization requires determining the cycle time, elemental time, standard operations routine, standard quality of WIP, and the standard of performance. The starting point is determining the cycle time that must be met to satisfy production requirements.

The first step in achieving balanced manufacturing is to document present WIP inventory because it is a symptom of unbalanced operations. Once the levels of WIP inventory have been documented, the following questions need to be addressed:

1. Have setup time reductions been implemented? What is the potential for setup time reductions?
2. Have production lot sizes been reduced? What is the potential for production lot size reductions?
3. Has uncertainty been minimized? What potential exists for minimization of uncertainty?
4. Have focused departments and focused factories been implemented? What opportunities exist for the creation of focused departments and focused factories?
5. Do production lots continuously flow through manufacturing operations? Are all WIP inventory buffers justifiable? Are WIP inventory buffers high-turnover, low-inventory hesitations in the continuous flow of materials?
6. Have the proper procedures been put in place to maximize sequential flow? How can WIP inventory be reduced by implementing sequential flow?
7. Have standards of performance been established, accepted, and followed for each operation, focused department, and focused factory? How can the standards of performance be more rigorously pursued?
8. Have the operational costs of just-in-time been analyzed? Is there a proper understanding of the tradeoff between operating costs and balance?
9. Have capacity bottlenecks been properly analyzed? Has the issue of balance been properly addressed both before and after the capacity bottleneck?
10. If not already answered, why does WIP inventory exist? Are all WIP inventories justifiable?

No manufacturing operation will ever achieve total balance. Instead, your objective should be to achieve greater balance. Answering the questions above will allow you to prioritize opportunities; identify and evaluate alternatives; and define, approve, and implement improvement plans. Combining these activities with continuous improvement will lead to greater and greater balance.

Production and Inventory Control

The key elements of a successful, manufacturing synthesis production and inventory control system are:

1. **Future capable production and inventory control.** This is radically different from traditional production and inventory control. Production planning is more predictable because manufacturing and marketing work as a team, and product families will be produced at a much more uniform rate. Product development is an integrated, iterative process with more standard components. Continuous flow manufacturing is the norm. Production schedules are met because uncertainty is reduced and balance is greater.

2. **Straightforward and transparent production and inventory control.** Production and inventory are controlled by defining the products, families, and options to be produced; defining the volumes to be produced; specifying a production plan; defining when materials and capacity should be present; scheduling material delivery from vendors and focused factories; and monitoring schedule adherence.

3. **Theory of Constraints (TOC)-based production and inventory control.** TOC is a management philosophy. It is based on the key premise that only a few work centers control the output of an entire factory for each product line and that managing these Capacity-Constraining Resources (CCRs), or bottlenecks, maximizes the output of the factory. TOC utilizes the drum-buffer-rope method to schedule the flow of materials with an eye to market demand and reducing inventory and operating expenses. The drum, or constraint, sets the pace of the system; the buffer is the protective window of time that ensures that the drum never runs dry; and the rope is the schedule that releases materials in a synchronous manner that assures smooth material flow. By determining the performance limits for all production processes (i.e., recognizing bottlenecks), organizations utilizing the TOC methodology can see the following results: improved quality and increased throughput.

The results of these elements are vendor and focused-department schedules. Adherence to these schedules results in production and inventory control.

Inventories

Reducing inventories begins with documenting present levels of inventory. These levels should then be compared with whatever industry benchmarks are available. Factors to consider in determining the levels of inventory include industry norms, production constraints, seasonality, customer requirements, material availability, and production stability. After these factors have been considered, specific inventory reduction goals should be established. An inventory reduction team should then conduct an audit to determine why the present levels of inventory exist; this audit should also factor in the 12 Requirements of Success for the Future Capable Company. After considering the goal, the audit, the Requirements of Success, and the cost tradeoffs, the team can establish and implement specific recommendations to reduce inventory.

Reducing inventories allows organizations to focus on the problems that created the need for them. Full attention can be given to the problems because excessive inventories do not exist in manufacturing synthesis and, therefore, problems can be identified and solutions found quickly. Eliminating inventories makes it easier to maintain little or no inventory, which creates continuous flow, which leads to manufacturing synthesis.

Why Manufacturing Synthesis Is a Core Competency of Supply Chain Excellence

Manufacturing synthesis focuses on the fact that long lead-times make it impossible to plan and control priorities. Shorter lead-times clear the shop floor of WIP inventory, conflicting manufacturing priorities, and other manufacturing problems. The results are reduced inventories, quicker customer response, higher levels of employee satisfaction, higher quality products, lower manufacturing costs, and the ability to synchronize supply with demand.

When the requirements of manufacturing synthesis are applied to the supply chain, the result is manufacturing for Supply Chain Excellence. Manufacturing for Supply Chain Excellence is synchronized, streamlined, straightforward, responsive, flexible, modular, and continuously improving to create agility. It responds to change and integration quickly and easily because of these characteristics. It is a time-based competitive approach to BTO that integrates both internal and external manufacturing resources to maximize customer satisfaction. It also allows customization, which often is a result of or a companion to BTO.

An organization that has successfully applied manufacturing synthesis in its internal operations can use the same methodology for applying synthesis across the supply chain. This is why manufacturing synthesis is a core competency of Supply Chain Excellence.

12

Distribution Synthesis

"Efficiency is not enough. Agility is the key."

— Cranfield School of Management

A basic distribution system consists of four points connected by a transportation system. The four points are:

- Raw material supplier
- Manufacturing/assembly operation
- Warehouse
- End-user

Who and what the end-users are, where the raw materials are, and how raw they are depend on relative positions in the supply chain. A shirt-sewing operation sees the cutting operation as the supplier of raw material and the consumer as the end-user. The cutting operation sees the fabric mill as the raw material supplier and the sewing operation as the end-user.

This example of limited visibility is one of the limitations of a traditional distribution system. It fails to understand that each part of a supply chain is as important as the whole because one bad step can shut down the entire supply chain. To prevent this from happening and, at the same time, achieve Supply Chain Excellence, all distribution functions must work as one, with each function being equally aware of others. In other words, the supply chain must have an integrated approach to distribution. That is distribution synthesis

As I stated in Chapter 9, distribution synthesis is making sure that the right manufacturing operations and right distribution centers (DCs) are in the right locations holding the right amount of inventory and that the right transportation is being used to fulfill the order to the satisfaction of the customer. When this is done from a link's perspective, it is called logistics. When it is done from a chain's perspective—with No Boundaries—the results are reduced inventory investments, reduced distribution costs, improved customer satisfaction, and a streamlined, agile flow of goods to the marketplace.

Distribution synthesis requires removing barriers between warehousing and transportation until there are No Boundaries, accomplishing that by using a hybrid push/pull system that adjusts to more demanding customer satisfaction requirements. The foundation for distribution synthesis is a Distribution Strategic Master Plan (DSMP). This chapter explains the process of a DSMP; explains third party logistics; compares push, pull, and hybrid push/pull systems; and describes why distribution synthesis is a core competency of Supply Chain Excellence.

Distribution Strategic Master Plan

Strategic planning is the process of deciding an organization's objectives, fine-tuning them, determining the resources needed to attain those objectives, and establishing the policies to govern the acquisition, use, and disposition of resources. The objective of distribution strategic planning is to define the overall approach to stocking points, transportation, inventory management, customer satisfaction, and information systems and the way they relate in order to provide the maximum return on investment. A DSMP, therefore, comprises a strategic distribution network plan, a strategic warehouse plan, and a strategic transportation plan.

Factors Influencing the DSMP

Since distribution is a dynamic environment, business issues such as the global marketplace, the level of government involvement, the environment, and the issue of energy challenge it. At the same time, customers' requirements to increase pace, variety, and adaptability while reducing prices must be understood. All these issues raise the internal pressures on distribution to centralize, utilize third parties, improve information systems, increase productivity, and more fully utilize people.

The only way to survive a rapidly changing distribution environment is to have good strategic plans that address the future needs of distribution and the capabilities needed to be agile in distribution. Those plans need to accommodate factors that include:

The Value of Centralization — International Rectifier

Recently, International Rectifier, a manufacturer of electronic components for companies such as Ericsson and Motorola decided to move all its manufacturing out of Europe to various worldwide locations—including Mexico, the U.S., Singapore, Italy, and China-to take advantage of cost efficiencies in those countries. This meant closing all regional and local distribution sites and establishing all finished goods distribution from warehouse locations attached to the manufacturing sites. Customer expectations for timely and effective distribution, coupled with internal requirements for continuous cost improvements in the supply chain led to a set of distribution parameters around 60-hour delivery with a minimum of 98 percent on-time performance, and globally competitive pricing.

As a result of this decision, the supply chain was extended geographically, challenging its effectiveness. To achieve its corporate goal of continually reducing logistics costs, it was vital for International Rectifier's supply chain to be working at optimum efficiency. The company needed to eliminate direct distribution from the manufacturing location to the customer. Basically, this required changing the way International Rectifier's supply chain functioned. The result was the creation of a European hub at London's Heathrow Airport for finished goods from all over the world.

Among the numerous features of the hub are a 60-hour, door-to-door service from all sites in Mexico, the U.S., Singapore, Italy, and China, and a full track-and-trace down to box level on a Web site designed specifically for the customer and providing full visibility of the goods at all stages of the supply chain. A 98 percent service-level agreement is also in place. Daily activity and invoice reports are generated and distributed electronically to all parties, and performance reports are produced for quarterly global review meetings.

All goods are now shipped to the hub and distributed from there to European customers, creating efficiencies and volume benefits of shipments to the hub without establishing inventory holding positions within the pipeline. Since the hub became operational, lead-times and logistics costs have been reduced by 50 percent and 15 percent respectively, even though the supply chain now covers a wider geographic area. — Exel Case Study, Exel, plc

- Global marketplace—In today's world there is no choice but to understand the global strategy implications of all distribution decisions. The world's trading patterns are shifting, and this changes the distribution requirements, alters the location and number of warehouses, increases supply chain inventories, and creates new transportation opportunities and problems.

- Government involvement—Governments have deregulated transportation. It is important to understand that, just as government involvement has an impact on distribution, distribution leadership has an obligation to have an impact on government.
- Reverse distribution—An issue that is closely tied to the issue of government involvement is reverse distribution. Reverse distribution has two aspects. One is returned goods —returning a product back up the supply chain. The second is the task of recovering packaging and shipping materials and backhauling them to a central collection point for recycling. Handling the mechanics of reverse distribution requires significant attention.
- Off-highway vehicles—In the U.S., the Environmental Protection Agency is pushing to regulate off-highway vehicles. The internal combustion lift trucks that will be sold in the future will need to meet much stricter emission standards, but in many applications, electric vehicles will replace them.
- Energy—The cost of energy is a major concern for transportation companies. In the U.S, 60 percent of all energy consumption is for transportation. Although these costs tend to be buried in the overall cost of transportation, any significant shift in the cost of energy could have an impact on the costs of transportation and therefore on distribution. It is therefore important that, at least as a sensitivity issue, energy costs be considered in all distribution decisions.
- Pace—The rate of change is accelerating in all aspects of human endeavor—social, political, economic, technological, ecological, and psychological. It is not surprising, then, that reduced lead-times, shorter product lives, and increased inventory turnover are resulting in significant increases in the pace of change in distribution. Distribution must be more responsive to customers' demands.
- Variety—The variety of tasks handled by distribution continues to increase. Special packaging, unitizing, pricing, labeling, kitting, and detailed delivery requirements are becoming the norm. Distribution must perform operations that traditionally have been viewed as manufacturing operations. Systems and procedures will be put in place to handle information consistent with the desires of the customers.
- Flexibility—The most important aspect of flexible distribution is versatility—in equipment, systems, and workers. Designing, specifying, and implementing versatile equipment are required to achieve flexible distribution. Warehouse storage rack and material handling equipment as well as transportation equipment should be selected with sufficient versatility to handle today's distribution requirements and, when justifiable, future requirements. Similarly, versatile systems adapt to customer labeling, automatic identification, communications, and documentation requirements. We never want to find

ourselves saying to a customer, "I am sorry, our system does not allow us to accommodate your request."

- Modularity—The three most important aspects of modular distribution are modular distribution assets, modular work assignments, and time modularity. The issue of modular distribution assets has to do with expanding and contracting warehouse space and increases or decreases in transportation equipment. Similarly, for transportation equipment, purchase and lease decisions as well as contract terms should be evaluated when considering long-term and short-term fluctuations in traffic.

- Price—A prerequisite for the success of free enterprise is efficient, effective, and low-cost distribution. Although the cost of distribution is less than 10 percent of the price the customer must pay, it is of the utmost importance to the customer that even this price be reduced.

- Centralization—Fewer and larger centralized warehouses have replaced more numerous, smaller, decentralized warehouses of the past. Fewer managers and administrative people are involved with distribution as integrated distribution is pursued and staff is centralized. Along with the centralization of warehouses and staffs comes the centralization of order entry, customer service, and data processing. Centralized distribution results in higher inventory turnover, which will, in turn, lead to new opportunities for automation and sophisticated information systems.

- Third-party logistics—Third-party logistics (3PL) is utilizing an outside firm to perform some or all distribution functions. Now that companies have greater understanding of integrated distribution and distribution leadership has greater understanding of distribution costs, outsourcing is on the rise.

- Information systems—It has become clear that all distribution documentation must be electronic. Distribution paperwork needs to be scrutinized and eliminated whenever possible. It is important to realize that paperwork means delays, errors, additional work and, therefore, wasted time and money. Distribution information systems must be real-time and paperless and standardized throughout the distribution supply chain.

- Productivity—Accountability for performance in distribution must be increased, which means establishing standards, identifying opportunities for improvement, measuring performance, and taking action to assure continuous distribution improvement. Most importantly, productivity must increase. Maintaining the status quo is totally unacceptable.

It is important to consider all these factors in a strategic distribution master plan.

A DC That Meets Customer Needs— Master Lock

Milwaukee-based Master Lock has had its ups and downs over the years, but a recent a re-engineering project that included opening a new DC in Louisville, Kentucky, and turning it into much more than just a pick, pack and ship center, has the company riding a wave of success. For example, Master Lock had begun offering more product colors, sizes and configurations based on customer needs, so it decided to put in place a postponement strategy for packaging. To delay packaging until the last moment, Master began building product in bulk and packaging it at the DC.

Because of this and other new strategies, the new DC was outfitted with three high-speed ultrasonic welding sealers in the light assembly and manufacturing area. The result was the versatility to seal high volumes of fast-turning items, which allows the facility to maintain reduced lead-times in a pack-to-order and pack-to-stock environment. Also added were three similar sealers designed for lower-volume versatility so the DC could handle lower-volume specialty items or packaging combinations.

To enhance the DC's distribution functions, the company added high-speed conveyors that can move up to 1,500 cases per hour. The conveyors are equipped with two automated packing stations for labeling and packing less-than-case quantities. To make sure the staff was up to speed on the variety of tasks needed for the processes, a training program was put into place when the facility opened.

The result? Master Lock has been able to double throughput and decrease lead-times. Some 600 orders are shipped daily, with 99 percent of orders shipping within 24 hours, and 25 percent of all orders shipped same day. This compares with a four- to five-day turn at the former DC in Milwaukee. — *Warehousing Management,* June 1, 2002

Strategic Distribution Network Plan

The first step of the DSMP is a strategic distribution network plan. The objective is to determine a plan that indicates the most economical way to ship and receive product while maintaining or increasing customer satisfaction. Strategic distribution network planning typically answers the following:

• How many DCs should exist?
• Where should the DC(s) be?

- How much inventory should be stocked at each?
- What customers should each DC service?
- How should the customers order from the DC?
- How should the DCs order from vendors?
- How frequently should shipments be made to each customer?
- What should the satisfaction levels be?
- What transportation methods should be utilized?

Strategic distribution network planning also considers future distribution requirements. To document the future distribution network requirements, it is important not only to understand the factors influencing distribution, but also to understand the marketing strategies and sales forecast. Are any new products being developed? If they are, what is the target market area? Are sales increasing each year? Are customer shifts or geographic shifts becoming apparent?

One of the key data items in analyzing a distribution network is delivery requirements (time from order placement to receipt of the shipment). If the requirements are not identifiable, a customer satisfaction gap analysis must be undertaken. The gap analysis is a series of questions directed at staff and customers to identify discrepancies between customer perception of satisfaction and satisfaction requirements. The key is to find the best service that maximizes profits.

The process looks at all the alternatives for a distribution network and determines which is optimal. With that decision made, the next step is to compare the recommended network plan with the implementation cost. To do this analysis, you must determine all the investments and savings associated with each alternative, then do a sensitivity analysis that varies different costs and savings to see which alternatives are the most stable and should be performed. To round out the analysis, a qualitative analysis should be performed looking at such factors as customer satisfaction and ease of implementation. Once a conclusion has been reached, a time-phased implementation schedule should be drawn up listing the major steps involved in transferring the distribution network from the existing system to the future system.

The final step in distribution network planning is selling the results to top management so they understand the impact of the strategy on the total business. Not only should this communication express the finances related to transportation and warehouse costs, but overall sales and customer satisfaction as well.

Warehouse Strategic Master Plan

The second requirement for a DSMP is a warehouse strategic master plan. Warehousing is a dynamic, continuously evolving environment in which the current plans and operations are constantly being scrutinized and molded to meet current and anticipated requirements. A successful warehouse maximizes the use of its resources while satisfying customer requirements; therefore its place in the DSMP is critical, since customer satisfaction depends on how the warehouse is designed, laid out, and utilized.

A warehouse's resources are systems/equipment, space, and personnel. Systems/equipment refers to information technology, dock equipment, material handling equipment, and unit load equipment. These comprise a large capital investment and must be selected and used so that the end result is an acceptable Return on Investment (ROI). Space costs include the cost of investment or lease and operating expenses, which includes taxes, insurance, maintenance, and energy. Personnel are the third resource. Approximately 50 percent of the costs of a typical warehouse are labor-related. Reducing the amount of labor and pursuing higher labor productivity will significantly reduce warehouse operating costs.

A warehouse strategic master plan is a set of documents describing actions to be accomplished and when they must be accomplished to satisfy the warehousing requirements of an enterprise over a given planning horizon. A closer examination of this definition reveals the important attributes of a good warehouse strategic master plan.

First of all, a good warehouse strategic master plan is a formal set of documents. They commonly include an implementation plan, a descriptive narrative, scaled facility drawings, supporting economic cost and justification data, and a specified planning horizon. The horizon should have a definite beginning and ending point and is typically stated in terms of years.

The strategic master planning process will not be complete unless the warehouse pursues continuous improvement by customizing; maximizing effective use of space, equipment, and labor; and maximizing the accessibility and protection of the product. Therefore, the warehouse must provide the following services:

- Customizing generic products in the warehouse (on-demand packaging)
- Compliance labeling
- Ticketing and bagging
- Dunnage
- Palletization

In other words, the warehouse is evolving into a "customer satisfaction center" that performs numerous customized and value-added services to products before shipment. This has created changes in four areas:

- Facilities—Due to manufacturing producing generic product, manufacturing is being simplified and the amount of space required for finished goods is being reduced. At the same time, the warehouse needs more storage and working space for customization activities.
- Equipment—New, different equipment is required for customized warehousing as a result of changing storage requirements and the addition of some manufacturing functions to the warehouse.
- Technology—To handle the demands of customization, the warehouse needs a real-time, barcode-based WMS that uses radio frequency communication and has the functionality to kit materials, schedule production tasks, and track work-in-progress.
- Labor—Depending on the specific, customized warehousing design, more labor may be required. Even if no additional labor is necessary, however, the needed skill sets are changing and production workers are being transferred from manufacturing to the warehouse.

Warehouses are no longer in reactive mode. They have adopted proactive processes for handling customization trends. In other words, their paradigm has shifted. Today's warehouse requirements must apply not only to the finished-goods function, but also to the manufacturing, raw material and WIP functions. This may be accomplished through restructuring the functions of manufacturing warehousing.

Transportation Strategic Master Plan

The third step in the DSMP is the transportation strategic master plan. It begins with gathering information from all supply chain partners on freight classes and discounts, transportation operating procedures, and replenishment weight/cube. Then, determine delivery requirements, counting the time from order placement to the receipt of the shipment. If the requirements are not identifiable, conduct a customer satisfaction gap analysis like that described in the strategic distribution network plan section. Build a database that includes ship-to locations, weight of shipments, products ordered, and quantity ordered, and have supply chain partners validate it.

Consider all transportation alternatives, including consolidating vendor shipments, centralizing slow-moving items in one place, and establishing direct shipment by vendors. Today, carriers are providing more services and trying to break into new markets (e.g. intermodal services, containerization, import/export). When considering transportation, organizations must leverage their buying and negotiating clout to get the best rates and service possible.

With the information in-hand, build a computer model of the costs, work up alternative plans, and select the best design that meets the requirements. Like the other two strategic planning processes, a transportation strategic master plan is never complete. It must be constantly updated and changed to meet the changes in the marketplace and the challenges of distribution today.

Implementing the DSMP

Implementing the DSMP means translating it into a working system. Implementation is like a train. It starts slowly with no seeming sense of urgency, but quickly picks up momentum. If not properly managed, it can get out of control. Implementation requires a high degree of respect for today's distribution challenges. These are discussed in the following sections.

Challenges in Distribution

It was once believed that to improve customer satisfaction, it was necessary to maintain high levels of finished goods inventory to prevent stock-outs. Although customer satisfaction levels may have been met, the actual competitiveness of an organization probably deteriorated because of higher inventory levels, resulting in increased carrying costs and decreased cash flows. Why? Generally it is because of three conditions. First, there is too much of the right inventory; second, there is too much of the wrong inventory; and third, the warehouse space is poorly utilized. To address each type of space issue appropriately, one must first understand the issues.

Having an abundance of the right product appears positive in terms of customer satisfaction and order fulfillment goals. Yet, as the sales staff and buyers celebrate, the warehouse operates well below established productivity and safety standards. Pallets of product are stored in aisles, stacked in dock areas, and placed on rack end caps. Or, multiple SKUs of the product are mixed in single bin locations. Blocked visibility creates safety hazards and decreases labor productivity, while inefficient multiple handling of product becomes an accepted practice. However, the right product usually moves quickly through the warehouse and space problems exist for short periods.

Too much of the wrong product often indicates that sales projections or production planning are incorrect. It also often indicates that the warehouse is not managing inventory levels or obsolete product properly. Unlike having too much of the right product, where short inventory peaks can be dealt with using extra labor, having the wrong product requires management actions to resolve the problem. If not, the inventory remains in the warehouse for months or even years. A good example of this lack of inventory management occurred at the warehouses of a mid-size arts and crafts supplier. Upon reaching a full warehouse condition at both its manufacturing and distribution centers, the company brought in a consultant who, upon examination, discovered that 600 of the 3,000 pallets at the manufacturing center had not been used in the last 12 months. At the distribution center, over 400 of the 4,500 pallets on-hand had no movement in over three years and another 500 pallets had zero activity within 12 months. Too much of the wrong product was solved with the stroke of a pen and a one-time hit to the bottom line.

Poorly utilized space, a condition usually caused by growth and changing storage and service requirements, is common and does not depend on inventory type or storage conditions in the warehouse. Traditionally, warehouses are built and equipped to handle projected volumes, a set number of products, and limited unit loads. Then they are expected to adjust to customer demands and be more efficient as time passes. To handle these conflicts, warehouses generally accept long-term penalties. Examples include creating customized floor-ready merchandise for end cap displays and hand-pricing a key customer's merchandise on the piece level when goods traditionally ship in full-case quantities. Both of these actions take valuable floor space and labor away from primary warehouse functions.

Another challenge is the combination of marketing and its impact on SKU proliferation, and manufacturing and its desire to maintain long production runs. This combination can easily hinder all attempts to improve the distribution function. The final challenge lies in meeting management's desire to have the lowest-cost distribution network with maximum customer satisfaction and high inventory turns. To fully synchronize supply and demand, manufacturing synthesis must build to order, and distribution synthesis must deliver with speed to the customer.

Individually, each of the three management desires is advantageous. In combination, however, they actually defeat one another. For example, maximum customer satisfaction for an organization might require a network of 10 DCs fed by three supply sources, but this network will invariably require more inventory and cost more to operate than a network of three DCs. The real goals in distribution are to establish a level of customer satisfaction that meets or exceeds the customer's expectations and to minimize inventories and reduce costs. Once the customer satisfaction levels have been set, an organization must then rethink its distribution strategy and consider third-party logistics, the push system vs. the pull system, and improved transportation management.

Third Party Logistics

Third party logistics (3PL) can be defined simply as using others to provide all or a portion of the logistics function. 3PL can offer flexibility, relieve frustration in managing non-core competencies, save money, and reduce inventory. However, 3PL can also reduce flexibility, contribute to frustration in core competency areas, cost money, and increase inventory. In other words, all outsourcing is not created equal.

The three basic categories for 3PL provider competencies are: asset-based, management-based (also called non-asset-based), and integrated operators. Asset-based 3PL providers offer a dedicated logistics service through use of their assets, including trucking operations, private fleets, warehouses, and so forth. Management-based providers focus on the management and technological services associated with providing logistics services. In most cases, these providers utilize the assets and the manpower of other organizations to provide logistics services and do not own transportation or warehousing assets. Integrated providers typically are outgrowths of a contract or for-hire logistics services and supplement their services with other vendors' offerings.

While evaluating 3PL in your DSMP, it is vital to collect information about your operation, document it in a request for proposal, evaluate each candidate thoroughly, and use quantifiable criteria for choosing the appropriate 3PL provider if that is the correct course. If 3PL is a good choice, the 3PL provider should be treated as a partner, with emphasis on communication, performance incentives, and a mutually agreeable contract.

Push vs. Pull Systems

Push systems are the byproducts of mass production. In a push system, sales predictions are used to determine the quantity of products to be produced and where they should be shipped. Forecasts are developed for sales regions, and products are manufactured and sent to the regions based on these forecasts. The emphasis is on using information about customers, suppliers, and production to manage material flow. In other words, the system

3PL Outsourcing Criteria

Quantifiable criteria that may be used to evaluate 3PL candidates include:

- Customer satisfaction—Check references and perform site visits to both the provider candidate and its customers. Will the third party provider seek and use input from your customers to improve the level of satisfaction? Will the provider be able to maintain and exceed current levels of satisfaction?
- Warehouse management systems—Does the provider use information technology to operate its business effectively? Can it develop, install, and operate a better system than the one you are currently using? How will your system and theirs be integrated?
- Flexibility—Can, and will, the provider change with your needs and your customer's needs?
- Buildings/facilities—Consider the availability, location, and utilization of dock capacity, lighting, personnel services, fire protection, and outside services
- Financial depth—Does the candidate have excellent credit and bank references? Is the financial statement solid?
- Geographic location—How does the candidate's geographic location make it strategically advantageous?
- Personnel depth—Is there sufficient expertise and quantity to keep your company well-serviced?
- Continuous improvement philosophy—Is continuous improvement embraced and practiced at every level of the operation?
- Cost—How does the cost of service compare with other candidates of equal capability?

pushes material through production according to schedules. Material is pushed from the production facility through distribution until the product reaches the customer.

Push systems depend heavily on the accuracy of forecasts. The advantages of a push system include:

- Smaller manufacturing plant warehouses because the only warehousing activity performed at the manufacturing facility is staging
- Enhanced customer satisfaction as products are pushed to locations close to the customer
- Shipments from the plant to DCs in truckload (TL) quantities, which creates lower transportation costs.

The biggest disadvantage of a push system is that it is based on regional forecasts, which are often inaccurate and many times unreliable. Bad forecasts can create

- Increased safety stock and, therefore, higher carrying costs
- Larger DCs to accommodate increased safety stock
- High stock-transfer costs due to increased material handling, shipping, product loss, and damaged material
- Reduced product rotation
- Reduced crossdocking capabilities.

A pull system functions most effectively in an environment with a variety of production and distribution points and a large number of SKUs in the system. In a pull environment, an order from a customer generates an order from the DC, which then leads to a production run to replenish the plant warehouse. Pull systems provide the capability to synchronize supply and demand. In a pull distribution system, an inaccurate sales forecast has a less significant impact on the distribution system for two reasons. First, the forecast is not required within a regional area, only at the global level. Actual customer demands at the DC level trigger replenishment activity from the plant. Second, all fluctuations in demand are corrected by changing the production schedule at the production source, not at the regional DCs.

However, a pull may experience significant potential problems including the following:

- Large on-site plant warehouses
- Slow order fill-time (lower customer satisfaction level)
- Increase in less-than-truckload (LTL) shipments.

The larger onsite plant warehouses occur because inventory is stored at the point of origin rather than at the point of distribution, as in a push system. These onsite plant warehouses increase the size of the plant and the plant warehouse staff, although they may eventually be beneficial because they provide space into which production could expand in the future. One way to reduce the size of the onsite warehouse is to shorten the production runs by synthesizing manufacturing. In general, the investment in production equipment to increase capacity, improve efficiency, reduce maintenance, and reduce changeover time is better than investing in warehouse space. One way to reduce the impact of slow order fill-time is by synthesizing distribution.

A slower order fill time reduces the customer satisfaction level. As orders take longer to reach the customer, the future sales growth may slow or even decrease. Balancing the lead-time for customer orders, inventory to fill those orders, and manufacturing lot sizes becomes extremely critical to limit the potential for lost sales.

The final potential penalty occurs when customer orders are placed. The combined demand for orders in a region generally does not equal full truckload (TL) quantities. To increase the number of TL shipments, additional orders need to be batched, which will further reduce response times. When orders cannot be combined to create TL quantities to a DC, the transportation cost of an order increases significantly. Eliminating stock transfers between DCs, as occurs in a push system, may offset this additional cost, however.

Nonetheless, now that sales forecast inaccuracies have less impact on a pull system, the following benefits can be realized:

- No stock transfers between DCs
- Lower safety stock
- Lower overall system inventory
- Direct plant-to-customer shipment opportunities.

The buffer inventory maintained at the plants serves as the system inventory and handles the reallocation of products to the DCs when sales fluctuations occur. This eliminates DC-to-DC stock transfers. In addition, by storing all the inventory at the plants, the safety stock is reduced, because only system-wide sales fluctuations, rather than regional and system-wide sales fluctuations, affect product inventory. This in turn reduces the overall system inventory and the required warehouse space.

The final benefit of a pull system comes from the opportunity for shipments to be made directly from the plant to the customer. For large customer orders from one plant, that plant can ship the order directly to the customer. This reduces costs of transportation and handling, reduces DC traffic, and improves response time and customer satisfaction.

Hybrid Push/Pull System

In theory, Supply Chain Excellence requires a pull system in which supply and demand are synchronized. In reality, a hybrid, or synthesized, push/pull system is more likely to contribute to achieving Supply Chain Excellence because it can level manufacturing loads and address seasonality and peaks. A synthesized distribution system utilizes the push system for more popular SKUs and the pull system for slower-moving ones. Consequently, slower-moving SKUs are either made to order or stored at the production facility, and the more popular SKUs are transported in truckload quantities to DCs for distribution to customers.

The hybrid system has the following benefits over a push system:

- Reduction of stock transfers
- Reduction of safety stock
- Opportunities for direct-customer shipments
- Improved opportunities for crossdocking
- Utilization of full truckloads
- Improved customer satisfaction

An overall design strategy, therefore, requires both strategic and tactical refinements until the pull percentage is optimized.

Transportation Management

Today, carriers negotiate any level of discounting they want, unlike the days when the Interstate Commerce Commission established rates for them. Carriers are also free to act as:

- Common carriers
- Contract carriers
- Brokers
- Freight forwarders

They may act as several or all of these simultaneously, and suddenly, all the players on the field are wearing each other's uniforms. This is the same as Dan Marino acting as quarterback one moment and right tackle the next. This can create a type of distribution free-for-all.

Often, organizations try to increase control over their distribution expenses by reducing the number of carriers they use. This appears to be a smart idea, until the carrier goes on strike. To meet the challenges of transportation management, consider these guidelines:

- Specify free on-board, inbound freight. Ask suppliers for "freight collect" product costs in addition to prepaid freight charges. This will enable the buyer to analyze the logistics costs of items and will provide additional flexibility in negotiating price and service issues.

- Renegotiate rates and services if they're more than one year old. Many transportation providers are offering additional services and better rates to beat their competition. There is nothing to lose by testing the waters every year.

- Assess the current transportation philosophy of the organization. The "if it ain't broke, don't fix it" mentality just does not apply here. Have you considered containerization for freight transport, for example? Imagine the amount of product that can fill a 20-foot-equivalent unit. For that matter, imagine never having to use overnight/priority shipping because distribution has planned properly and made the right freight decisions. What you did yesterday or even this morning might not provide competitive advantage this evening.

- Shop till you drop. A carrier decision takes into account more than just rates. Other considerations are service, a solid track and safety record, and geographic coverage and evaluation of the provider's financial status. Use carriers as resources and springboards for ideas. Make sure you compare.

- Regard purchasing and sales as allies. By forging strategic alliances within the four walls of the organization, transportation can be part of the solution rather than part of the panic.

- Evaluate the third party logistics (3PL) concept for non-core competencies. If ware-housing and transportation functions are viewed as cost centers, 3PL might be the road to take.

- Remember that you are in business for your customer. One company I visited measured shipping errors as a function of customer complaint calls. A good day equaled a day with no calls. Unfortunately, the company didn't realize that no calls might have meant that the customer simply gave up on them and sought another supplier altogether. Being active with customers (e.g., creating surveys, calling them for feedback before they call you) rather than reactive serves to unite customer and company more completely.

In addition to these steps, management should periodically review those metrics that have been chosen to monitor the business to determine if they still represent current business practices or should be changed.

Why Distribution Synthesis Is a Core Competency of Supply Chain Excellence

The characteristics of distribution synthesis are:

- Understanding the importance of customer requirements and satisfaction when designing a distribution network
- A DSMP that defines the requirements for an efficient and effective distribution system
- Proper utilization of 3PL
- Economic and qualitative evaluation of all viable alternatives based on specific, weighted criteria before any distribution network decisions are made
- Use of a hybrid push/pull system of distribution to maximize customer satisfaction and optimize manufacturing efficiency
- Defining the most cost-effective supply chain solution to synchronize supply with demand

These characteristics generally indicate distribution synthesis for one organization. However, if a company has the knowledge to implement them internally, then that company has the knowledge to implement these characteristics for the entire supply chain. All distribution decisions (e.g., number and location of DCs, inventory levels, optimal order cycles and fulfillment rates, and order procedures) are then geared toward synchronizing, being agile, and achieving Supply Chain Excellence, rather than relying on SCM or a traditional logistics environment. That is why distribution synthesis is a core competency of Supply Chain Excellence.

13

Partnerships

"It is probably not love that makes the world go around, but rather those mutually supportive alliances through which partners recognize their dependence on each other for the achievement of shared and private goals."

— Fred Allen

There is lots of talk about "partnerships." The Internet, deregulation, deverticalization, and global competition are driving an explosion of so-called partnerships worldwide. In the summer of 2001, for example, a search for "partnerships" at www.manufacturing. net brought a list of articles that announced more than 200 new "partnerships," many of them trade exchanges or marketplaces for B2B commerce. About the same time, however, market researchers at International Data Corp. in Framingham, Massachusetts, estimated that fewer than 300 of 1,500 B2B "partnerships" that had been created were doing any business. So why does Supply Chain Excellence require partnerships if they don't last or don't work? It depends on what you mean.

Shakespeare asked, "What's in a name?" The answer is "not much" if that is all there is behind a partnership. While the Bard said a rose by any other name still smelled like a rose, many companies that are forming "partnerships" are not doing what needs to be done to take them and their supply chains through the levels of Supply Chain Excellence. Calling a relationship a "partnership" does not get it past being simply another name for a communication system with lots of information technology (IT) bells and whistles created simply to exploit the Internet and World Wide Web but without with any real plan or idea of what the partners wanted to accomplish for their supply chains.

The reason that many of these so-called partnerships failed and why more will fail is that they use technology and communications to foster traditional supplier/customer (manufacturer/wholesaler/retailer) relationships, not to bring new understanding of what supply chain partnerships must be. The same can been said about efficient consumer response (ECR). These relationships are not true partnerships.

In Chapter 10, I explained the three customer tiers and identified the highest tier of customers as partners. In other words, you want to create partnerships with them, because they are essential to agility, operational success, and continuous improvement.

Achieving the true partnerships needed for Supply Chain Excellence is somewhat like the dating that leads to marriage. There's a meeting, then a date, then more dates. There is the time when both partners decide that they only want to date each other. If all goes well, there is an engagement and a wedding date is set. If the engagement is a success, then the wedding takes place. This all takes time and it has to be done right. Suppose you go to a bar tonight and someone who hasn't met you before asks, "Hey, want to get married?" Most likely you would either think that person wasn't serious or that person was crazy. If you accept the proposal, then both of you are crazy.

Marriage does not end this process. Marriages continuously change and develop. I've been married for more than 34 years. The relationship my wife and I have is different now than it was 30 years ago. It has continued to evolve as we have evolved from a young couple to parents of two adults and a teenager. And it doesn't stop here. It will keep changing as long as we are both alive.

It also takes time to create the relationships that lead to true partnerships. They are not created over night and require a great deal of intimacy. The business equivalent of a couple dating is the move to a partnership with a "customer-driven" organization. The next step is invincible customer satisfaction, which is the business equivalent of "going steady." To move beyond this relationship, the partners must step up their commitments to one another. Then the partners must begin significant planning for the partnership, just as if they were planning a wedding. The ultimate commitment is a true partnership.

True partnerships have critical roles in Levels 2 through 6 of Supply Chain Excellence. Without true partnerships between departments, Link Excellence is nothing more than a dream. The sharing of information necessary for Visibility means eliminating adversarial customer/supplier relationships. Collaboration, which is based on trust between the collaborators, is not possible without true partnerships. Synthesis and Velocity also require true partnerships. They are necessary for ensuring customer satisfaction from the original raw material provider to the ultimate, finished-product consumer, and they use IT capabilities wisely, rather than blindly, to ensure quality communications.

Deverticalization —
Creating the Need for Partnerships

A jack of all trades and master of none—that is why a vertical organization does not contribute to Supply Chain Excellence as well as it should. Vertical organizations own more of their supply chains and therefore focus less on core competencies. This was an acceptable proposition in SCM, when link optimization was tantamount to supply chain success. For example, vertical food conglomerates own farms, processing plants, manufacturing facilities, and warehouses. Acquisitions were seen as an effective way of growing market share and profitability.

What do these conglomerates do best when they're highly verticalized? Consumed by doing everything in their niche, they forget what was really at the heart of their strategic plan and they achieve mediocrity in many areas with excellence in none.

Companies "deverticalize" by selling and outsourcing major supply chain segments while retaining control of their core business. Deverticalization can eliminate weak links in the supply chain and allow core divisions to grow, but it should never be done without a time-phased strategic action plan. An action plan enables a company to see the big picture of where it is headed and what functional strengths will take it to higher market share and competitive advantage.

What happens when deverticalization occurs exclusive of an action plan? Organizations tend to choose price but want high quality and wind up disappointed. Developing a master plan will certainly rein in the wheeler-dealers and enable the company to move in the direction of its strategic vision without hitting a lot of bumps in the road.

Not using a hand does not mean cutting it off, an analogy that holds true for companies that deverticalize. If a non-core competency is outsourced, organizations must audit performance of the third party regularly for continuous improvement. Supply chain partners must be held to a specific standard (e.g., supplier certification programs such as those enacted by AIAG, the Automotive Industry Action Group). No one has to forsake control over the quality of a function just because someone down- or upstream is doing it.

Peak-to-Peak Performance begins with defining core competencies. Highly verticalized conglomerates cannot label everything a "core competency" and expect to succeed in this changing business climate. Supply Chain Excellence begins with the notion that there are others in the supply chain who can perform functions better than you and inversely, who rely on you. This is why partnerships are so critical to Supply Chain Excellence.

This chapter defines true partnerships, discusses the challenges of true partnerships, gives the prerequisites to true partnerships, describes how to create a true partnership, and demonstrates why partnering is a core competency of Supply Chain Excellence.

True Partnerships

To understand true partnerships, you must keep these things in mind:

- When similar companies in the same kind of business band together to pool their resources to conduct research, evaluate technology, or lobby for a political position, they have not created a partnership. They have created a consortium.
- When companies lose their independence to become one corporate entity, it is not a partnership. It is an acquisition or merger.
- When companies work together to pursue a specific, single-focused business objective, this is not a partnership. It is a strategic alliance.
- When two companies form a separate entity with joint ownership to pursue a specific business objective, they have a joint venture, not a partnership.
- A long-term relationship based upon trust and a mutual desire to work together for the benefit of the other partner and the partnership is a true partnership.

As you can see, it takes two committed organizations to have a true partnership. Each true partnership requires a supplier and a customer who are both ready for partnership. True partners invest in the long-term partner relationship that is based on trust and a mutual desire to work together for the benefit of the other partner and the partnership; there are No Boundaries separating their abilities to share information and requirements. Both organizations in the partnership are interdependent, but each retains its own identity to assure maximum innovation and creativity.

The characteristics of a true partnership are

- The partners reject the "arm's length" mindset, i.e., that business relationships should be based on antagonism, leveraging, hammering, and negotiating.
- The partners are committed to long-term relationships based on trust and a true understanding of their partner's business. The partners believe in sharing of information, planning, scheduling, risk, rewards, problems, solutions, and opportunities.
- The partners believe in working together toward improvements in quality, lead-times, new product development time, inventory accuracy and management, and cost control.

Alliances Make Sense for Japanese Electronics Companies

The global economic slump has battered Japanese electronics companies. In an effort to shore up profits, Japanese electronics companies are turning to strategic alliances, especially in the chip sectors. Although Japan had a lead in low-end memory chips about 20 years ago, it has increasingly lost market share to emerging manufacturers from the rest of Asia such as South Korea's Samsung Electronics Co., which is reporting booming profits.

In March 2002, Hitachi and Mitsubishi Electric Corp. announced a joint venture to bring together their system LSI business, a relatively sophisticated kind of computer chip used in mobile phones and digital appliances. In April, IBM Corp., Sony Corp., and Sony's video-game unit, Sony Computer Entertainment, said they will jointly develop technologies with Toshiba for making advanced computer chips expected to be used in future electronics products. Then, in June 2002, Fujitsu and Toshiba Corp. announced that they were forming an alliance to create sophisticated computer chips in June 2002.

The Fujitsu-Toshiba alliance will allow both companies to share costs and bring together design teams to make a new kind of chip that better integrates software with circuitry. Demand for such chips is expected to grow as mobile homes, digital TVs, and some appliances connect to the Internet. Toshiba's strength in digital consumer products and Fujitsu's expertise in servers will complement each other. — AP, June 19, 2002

- The partners believe in building on each other's strengths, increasing their partner's business, and investing in the long-term partnership relationship. Due to this commitment, the partners will deal with fewer and fewer suppliers.
- The partners believe in systems integration and the interdependence of their organizations while still retaining their individual identities to assure innovation and creativity.
- The partners believe in frequent communications at all levels of the organization and that partnership proximity is important and will be mutually addressed.
- The partners believe in getting their partners involved early in any new innovations and working with their partners with the utmost flexibility to assure the best overall performance of the partnership.

In other words, true partnerships are long-term collaborative relationships based on trust and a mutual desire to work together for the benefit of the other partner and the partnership.

The Challenges of True Partnerships

Because a partnership is a true investment of time, money, and reputation, a lot is at stake. Forming a true partnership requires discarding the traditional relationships common between organizations today. In the traditional arrangement, limited communication flows vertically within the two companies. It moves between them only through the sales staff and buyers. Even then, the focus is usually on problems, not their causes, correction, or continuous improvement. These factors contribute to extended lead-times, higher costs, and a relationship that ignores the supplier's creativity.

Therefore, the key challenges to forming true partnerships exist in the areas of trust, communication, and organizational and cultural change. These challenges can be overcome. As more true partnerships are embraced in this millennium, such methods of overcoming challenges will become the norm.

Trust

Trust is the key ingredient in a partnership. Trust between partners takes time and happens as a result of many positive interactions. From trust, relationships grow, trust progresses to respect, and respect fosters the willingness to listen. From this listening comes understanding, concern, participation, and then open communication. Since open communication leads to positive reinforcement for even greater trust. Without trust, there is no partnership.

It is important to note that trust does not occur between companies, but between people. Therefore, partnerships are not really about companies, but about people-and those people must be committed to making a partnering relationship work, whether it is a marriage or a partnership between a supplier and a customer. When employees are viewed as people who are part of the whole process, when previously proprietary information is shared, and when everyone shares the benefits of success, then employees develop trust in the organization and the cycle of success continues. When this kind of trust is developed within an organization (organizational change), the employees are better prepared to apply the same kind of trust to their formerly antagonistic relationship with customers/suppliers (cultural change).

Communication

The success of partnering efforts depends on the effectiveness of communication. Today's technology enables an instantaneous, continuous flow of information within and between organizations, which is discussed in Chapters 14 and 15, but care must be taken not to

Trust in Partnerships—Magic Johnson

Earvin "Magic" Johnson, former L.A. Lakers basketball star turned businessman, has become the dream partner of several corporations. Johnson is a trusted partner in a joint theater venture with Loews Cineplex, in an alliance with Starbucks Coffee, in restaurant deals with T.G.I. Fridays and Fatburger, and in an equity investment in newly branded 24 Hour Fitness Magic Johnson Sports Club.

Travis Reid, the CEO of Loews, which together with Johnson Development operates five theaters with 60 screens across the country, says that Johnson stands for something that matters. "We think his personality not only represents a great basketball player, but a great role model who stands for giving back to the community," Reid said. "He brings the feeling that something is being done for the community and the community needs to support it. We've had nothing but a positive experience."

Johnson's involvement in the Loews chain is very active, from personal appearances to making sure each of his theaters caters to the minority communities where he builds, whether through "walls of fame" in theater lobbies saluting African-Americans or providing specialty items on the concession stand.

Johnson leaves the management of the theater and the negotiation of film terms up to Loews. With business partner and Johnson Development president Kenneth Lombard, he is instead responsible for generating advertising sponsorships and negotiating leases. Johnson counts General Motors, his former employer from his high school days in Lansing, Mich., as one of his largest sponsors. — *Hollywood Reporter,* July 1, 2002

place too much emphasis on this technology while ignoring human interaction. It is important to have frequent and planned face-to-face interactions within the company and between partners. There must, therefore, be specific points of contact between the companies and assurance that they are committed to keeping the lines of communication open and anticipate potential problems.

Organizational and Cultural Change

The biggest challenge in creating true partnerships is overcoming the existing paradigms of partnerships. These paradigms are the byproducts of organizational culture, which may be compared to a personality. For example, several years ago, Tompkins began working with clients on establishing partnerships. A major grocery chain retained us and expressed a desire to form partnerships with three firms who did private labeling for the chain. The first firm produced juice, and its leadership was progressive but cautious. The second firm produced jellies, syrups, and sauces, and its leadership was secretive and resistant. The third firm produced cookies, and its leadership was open and eager to participate.

Well, the results were predictably very mixed. The cookie firm established a very meaningful partnership that netted huge benefits to both our client and the cookie manufacturer. The juice firm also established a meaningful partnership with the grocery chain, and it netted huge benefits for our client and the juice producer. However, the partnership took twice as long to be established and took twice as long to net results. The jelly firm did not establish a partnership. In fact, the lack of trust between the firms resulted in the deterioration of their relationship, a decline in activity, and the reduction in profits to each.

What is so amazing about these three relationships is that the grocery chain and our process were consistent in all three situations. It was the cultures of the three firms that dictated different responses to our partnership initiative and, thus, a wide diversity in results. Culture is a key component of establishing partnerships and must be understood and developed to achieve results from them.

To overcome a traditional view of partnerships, there must be organizational and cultural change (i.e., the Revolution discussed in Chapter 8). This may be accomplished with a Business Process Continuous Improvement (BPCI) philosophy. BPCI is a leadership-driven process of collaboration that uses teams and a shared Model of Success to change company culture and operating style. Teams are created across job functions, product classes, and internal organizations to consolidate, integrate, and share organizational responsibilities. Once BPCI is used within one organization to achieve cultural change, then companies may use it to develop a joint Model of Success for forming a true partnership.

Prerequisites to Partnerships

CEO commitment and leadership are core ingredients for a true partnership. Only the CEO has the power to commit the resources to form partnerships and to break down the barriers to resistance. The CEO must foster a climate that allows the organization to define its relationships with its suppliers and customers in new, agile, and creative ways. The CEO and upper management must make decisions that support the philosophy of continuous improvement, and they must communicate this philosophy throughout their company as well as outside it. Any choice made based on price alone sends a clear message that, while the company may say it wants cultural change and partnerships, in reality, it is "business as usual."

Too often, leadership gives its commitment, only to be distracted by more short-term issues. When leadership focuses elsewhere, the partnership initiative frequently founders. The wavering of top leadership's attention is one of the most frequent reasons that partnering initiatives fail.

Another cause of partnering initiative failures is the tendency of leadership to proceed before the organization is ready. Frequently, once the initiative is identified, leaders often want to charge forward and make improvements immediately. They tend to want to launch an intense effort before everyone understands the initiative, much less before they become aligned with it. Leaders expect committed employees and committed suppliers to follow.

A better approach is to develop a strong consensus and necessary supporting structure at the top before beginning the improvement effort. Senior leadership needs to spend time off-site working through the issues. This allows all concerns to be discussed until there is near total acceptance of the initiative, scope of actions, necessary cultural changes, rewards and recognition, supporting systems, and the process of implementing the mission statement.

Another prerequisite for a true partnership is developing a succeed/succeed mindset for the partners. What has historically held back partnerships has been a succeed/fail (or win/lose) mindset. Those who have this mindset believe that they fail if the other party succeeds, and so they do not cooperate. They view their partners as opponents, not collaborators. In a succeed/succeed partnering mindset, the supplier is totally focused on helping the customer achieve success because the supplier believes that is the only way to succeed. Powerful relationships develop because suppliers and customers are focused on making each other successful.

The final prerequisite for true partnerships is for each organization to develop an internal team-based structure and then take it outside the organization. In fact, the partnering process can be thought of as the application of team-based development between organizations. Organizations with such a structure respond quicker to change and thus are truly able to collaborate to deliver quality and customer satisfaction at a lower cost. Team-based organizations make true partners because they are better equipped to respond to strategic opportunities.

Creating True Partnerships

A true partnership is the successful application of the collaboration process between organizations. The objective of creating true partnerships is to create the same synergy, agility, and synchronization between organizations that was created from the collaboration process within an organization. Striving to create long-term partnerships means first understanding that the term "relationship" is not synonymous with partnership. Growing a relationship into a partnership means realizing that:

- No two relationships develop the same way.
- Relationships evolve as comfortable bonds between individuals.
- A positive chemistry must exist between two parties to create a relationship.
- Partnerships evolve from understanding, hopes, dreams, and an anticipation of a bright future.
- Each party must know itself and understand what it seeks from the partnerships.
- Acceptance by indirectly involved parties (e.g., stockholders, government) is as important to the perpetuation of the partnership as acceptance by directly affected parties.
- The relationship, at its core, has interest in the well-being of each party as well as the well-being of the partnership.
- Expectations of how the relationship will develop must be articulated.
- Compatibility is key to a long-term relationship.

Identifying potential true partners should be based on the opportunity for additional contribution to profit over a five-year planning horizon. This applies to both a customer looking at its suppliers and a supplier looking at its customers. First, the focus should be on building trust, then on communicating clearly, and finally, on creating the Peak-to-Peak Performance discussed in Chapter 8. As these relationships continue, the escalation of trust, openness, and success will naturally lead to the sharing of Models of Success and strategic business plans.

Also part of the partnership process is chartering a Partnership Initiative Team. The purpose of this cross-functional team is to establish an official collaborative relationship, determine the objectives of the partnership, and develop a mutual plan for the partnership. As a result, the supplier/customer roles will become blurred until they have No Boundaries—first between individuals, then teams, then entire companies will be true partners. Without boundaries, the partners will act as a whole to improve, grow, and prosper, while still maintaining their own corporate identities.

Why Partnering Is a Core Competency of Supply Chain Excellence

You cannot have Supply Chain Excellence without true partnerships. As discussed above, true partnerships are based on the principle that sharing information openly, communi-

The Value of Partnerships— Pallet Management Systems

Pallet Management Systems specializes in asset recovery of non-standard pallets, servicing the building materials, fibers, chemical and plastics, and high-value electronic markets. Pallet Management Systems has 15 locations and 450 employees, and the key to the company's success is simply to take a relationship-oriented approach to each client account, focusing on long-term solutions for its customers rather than quick fixes.

Pallet Management Systems understands that outsourcing on the part of its clients requires recognition of non-core competencies, and the company approaches its partnerships in the same way. By partnering with 3PLs, plastic packaging manufacturers, and RFID/barcoding technology integrators, the organization can provide an entire solution to an asset-recovery issue.

For example, through partnerships with RFID vendors, Pallet Management Systems can help clients enable the supply chain more effectively, providing more upstream information real-time. Once the packaging or pallet reaches a certain value, it justifies closer tracking as it travels from one manufacturer to the road to the customer and back again. Product and packaging are linked through bar coding or electronic tags, and such information as how quickly it moves allows companies to plan asset recovery strategies based on proven trends, rather than on hypotheses.

cating requirements extensively, and involving alliances early in processes will provide competitive advantage and strength to an organization.

To achieve Supply Chain Excellence, the concept of true partnership must extend beyond the organization to the supply chain. There, the intimacy of a true partnership is among supply chain partners with win/win mindsets and team-based structures committed to achieving Supply Chain Excellence. They have determined specific criteria for evaluating the partnerships as well as potential new partners. They also know, as supply chain partners, that they have a long-term relationship that must provide mutual benefits through open communication, continuous improvement, a focus on the customer and the pursuit of the synchronization of supply with demand. Therefore, they communicate with one another on causes of problems, corrections, and continuous improvement, rather than on the problems themselves.

Supply chain partners also believe that the challenges they face in partnerships-trust, communications, and culture-must be overcome to secure competitive advantage; improved performance of the TOTAL supply chain is necessary through partnerships; partnership success requires integration, information, and interaction; and it is important to benchmark partnership activity for continuous improvement.

The key to the success of supply chain partnering is to assure alignment around shared goals. Building on the assumption that intra-organizational alignment has been achieved, the next step is to ensure that this spirit of cooperation and collaboration is extended throughout the supply chain. In other words, there must be a supply chain culture that creates and nurtures Peak-to-Peak Performance through teaming, true partnerships, and the proper use of IT and the Internet. That is why partnering is a core competency of Supply Chain Excellence. Without partnering, organizations cannot go beyond Level 2 on the journey to Supply Chain Excellence. With partnerships, a supply chain can achieve Levels 3, 4, 5 and 6. Partnerships are a prerequisite for achieving Supply Chain Excellence.

14

Communications for Supply Chain Excellence

"Today we have access to technology that greatly facilitates the exchange of information. We can share methodologies with supplier-partners in ways that just weren't possible five or ten years ago, which results in dramatically faster time-to-market."

— Michael Dell

When you set out to integrate business processes and disparate entities in the supply chain, you must communicate. It is vital to the success of all Supply Chain Excellence core competencies. If you communicate effectively and continually across the supply chain, with No Boundaries, then you will be agile and synchronized and achieve Supply Chain Excellence.

Today, organizations have a variety of options for communicating openly. The Internet, direct links, and virtual private networks (VPNs) that transport data over secure channels all connect people and information quickly, easily, and at a minimal cost. The World Wide Web is a place for dialogue and relationships and a medium in which to resolve differences between systems and platforms. Off the Web, Auto ID, communications technology, and business software allow the exchange of data between various applications. Companies have a wide range of information systems available to them for strategic, tactical, and technical purposes. These include:

- Accounting
- APS
- Budgeting
- Enterprise resource planning (ERP)

The Difference Between the Internet and the World Wide Web

There is a common misconception that the terms "Internet" and "World Wide Web" mean the same thing. They do not.

The Internet is a global network that connects millions of computers. In September 2002, one estimate put the number of Internet users worldwide at 605.6 million, and that number keeps growing. More than 100 countries are linked into exchanges of data, news, and opinions. Each Internet computer, called a host, is independent. Its operators can choose which Internet services to use and which local services to make available to the global Internet community.

The World Wide Web is a system of Internet servers that support specially formatted documents. The documents are formatted in a language called HTML (HyperText Markup Language) that supports links to other documents, as well as graphics, audio, and video files. In other words, users can jump from one document to another simply by clicking on the links. Not all Internet servers are part of the World Wide Web. Because of this, the World Wide Web should be viewed as a subset of the Internet. It is an ever-growing part of the Internet, but it will never be the same entity.

- Finance
- Fleet maintenance
- Forecasting
- Freight rate management
- Inventory management and control
- MES
- Order entry, processing, and management
- Procurement
- Production planning and control
- Sales force automation
- Transportation Management System (TMS)
- Warehouse Management System (WMS)

At one time, these systems, which are covered more fully in Chapter 15, would have operated separately. Integrating this technology would have been expensive. However, in the last few years, Web-based applications have emerged to serve the same functions and can integrate and communicate with other applications. For those who don't want to replace expensive software installations, applications known as middleware create ways to tie disparate programs and systems together through enterprise application integrators (EAI) and Web application servers. This is virtually eliminating the expense factor that figured so highly in previous attempts at technology integration.

This chapter discusses what kind of communication is necessary for Supply

Chain Excellence. It also introduces and relates the following to Supply Chain Excellence: electronic data interchange (EDI); business applications; extranets; and Collaborative Planning, Forecasting, and Replenishment (CPFR).

Communication for Supply Chain Excellence

The communication necessary for Supply Chain Excellence is simultaneous, instantaneous, and multi-directional to allow all supply chain partners to work at the same time rather than sequentially—in other words, to be synchronized. The focus is to ensure that the entire chain is working with agility as one entity. This eliminates inventory buffers and accelerates the flow of cash. It also allows dynamic demand and supply chain planning, which replaces the outdated practices of long-term forecasting. It makes strategic information available to all partners so that all are in touch with the customer, are aware of changing needs and trends, and can then respond in unison to these needs and trends.

These communications must be clear, relevant, open, and honest. All parties must be linked, and the information requirements of each must be integrated into the communication process; that is why the Internet and World Wide Web play key roles. Clear, concise, and ongoing communication is needed from the outset as well as a willingness to share key information and withhold nothing. At the same time, the equality and interdependence of the players must be recognized and accepted. Each has a leading role in one or more functional areas, no matter how they are interconnected. These basic communication principles must be maintained throughout all supply chain processes.

Important to the success of these communications is the elimination of information silos. Information must be shared throughout the supply chain's communications network. If information is not shared and accessible to all links in the supply chain, Supply Chain Excellence cannot be achieved. Systems must be able to manage and transmit all types of data along the supply chain to make sure all partners are receiving accurate, timely, and high-quality information. It is critical that these systems exploit the power of the Internet and World Wide Web, for that is what can achieve the communications necessary for achieving Supply Chain Excellence.

Although Internet/Web-linked information and communication systems are the most critical requirements, completely effective communications systems must also facilitate face-to-face and interpersonal communications to maintain the trust necessary for true information sharing and collaboration. This means intelligent participation in and management of person-to-person communications consistent with supply chain partner needs.

The Value of Communications—APL

For centuries, shippers have relied on multiple copies of bills of lading—each going to the various parties involved in shipments. That process is changing. The chief information officer of Singapore-based Neptune Orient Lines (NOL) is leading an effort to move the paper-based shipping business onto the Web. Since 1995, when he established the first Web site for NOL's American President Lines (APL), he and others have steadily transferred the transactions required to ship cargo via APL's 80-odd vessels to the Web.

The company now uses electronic bills of lading, online versions of the letters of credit required for insurance, and real-time rate quotes for specialized cargoes. Today, 38% of APL's customers conduct their business via online transactions, up from 8% in 1999. And 25% of APL's North American customers never see a paper bill of lading.

The reduction of paper-pushing means APL employees are not engaged in repetitive paper processes and can solve more problems or offer sales support. Over the past two years, APL has seen its shipping volume increase significantly while the cost of processing bills of lading has decreased 20%.

APL's customers are also benefiting from the company's move to Web communications. APL has set up a Web interface that allows customers to view the status of their cargo shipments and request notification when a shipment is delayed or a problem arises. — BusinessWeekOnline, April 16, 2002

Building a communications system focused on achieving Supply Chain Excellence requires integrating three essential types of capabilities. The system must be able to handle day-to-day communications and transactions and e-commerce along the supply chain, which can help synchronize supply and demand because orders and daily schedules are shared. The system must also facilitate planning and decision making, supporting demand and shipment planning necessary for distributing resources effectively. And finally, the system must provide tools like an integrated network model that will allow strategic analysis. Electronic connectivity via the Internet or World Wide Web provides the backbone for this communications system, which will greatly reduce transaction costs as orders, invoices, and payments are handled electronically and reduce inventories through vendor-managed inventory programs. The key is ensuring the continuous flow of information.

Five Supporting Technologies of Supply Chain Communications

Five supporting technologies that add value, accuracy, and expediency to supply chain communications are:

- Direct Link—Telephoning and faxing are the most prevalent examples of direct link. More accurate, faster, and cheaper methods of information-sharing, involving less employee time and no paper shuffling, are outpacing direct link, but no one is predicting the end of voice communication quite yet.
- Local Area Networks (LANs)—Capable of transmitting data faster than telephony but over shorter distances, LANs let users share expensive peripheral devices such as printers. LANs also enable users to send e-mails and engage in chat sessions. The number of users on a LAN is limited, but many LANs connected to one another can form a WAN.
- Wide Area Networks (WANs)—A system of LANs connected via telephone lines and radio waves makes up a WAN, which can span a large geographic area. Computers typically connect to a WAN through telephone systems, leased lines, or satellites. The largest WAN in the world is the Internet.
- Virtual Private Networks (VPNs)—A network accessible only to users with authorization. VPNs guarantee security through encryption (translation of data into a secret code) and other security mechanisms. An example of a VPN in use is entering a confidential password that allows you access to your account on a large site such as Amazon.com. VPNs are usually connected to the Internet, but operate separately from it. To be a part of this network, companies must pass comprehensive and rigorous security tests.
- Electronic Data Interchange (EDI)—Once a competitive advantage enjoyed only by large companies that could afford it, EDI is becoming more accessible, courtesy of the Internet. A protocol for the electronic exchange of business documents in standardized format between businesses, major corporations use EDI for global communications with their trading partners. EDI has 300 transaction sets, three of which are purchase orders, invoices, and order acknowledgments. With its approved set of standards, called X12, EDI facilitates sharing of data between supply chain partners.

The Web is the great communications equalizer among organizations. Small companies with small company budgets are no longer faced with inaccurate communications, slow communications, or no communications. Companies do not even need T-1 lines (a popular leased line option for businesses connecting to the Internet) to be on top of their supply chain communications. They simply need a browser and an Internet Service Provider (ISP)

Migrating from EDI to the Web— Honda Motor Company

Honda Foundry, the unit of Honda responsible for manufacturing engine parts, has partnered with GE Global eXchange Services (GXS) for supply chain integration. GXS is contributing software to enable Honda Foundry to receive EDI orders over the Internet and convert them to various data formats compatible with its back-office systems. The goal of the implementation is to remove manual order-entry processes from Honda Foundry while also eliminating the need for customized alterations to its order processing systems.

Using GXS's data mapping and translation system, Honda Foundry continues to benefit from existing internal applications while it connects electronically to customers in new ways. Honda's decision to migrate EDI to the Web is an example of current enterprise thinking, which leans toward squeezing maximum value out of legacy investments before getting into new and potentially unproven technologies.

Jim Rogers, general manager of Integration Solutions at GXS, echoes this theme. "Enterprises want to continue and extend the use of systems already in place. We won't see complete investments to replicate what's already within the business." — Line 56, December 11, 2001

who understands their needs. The Web has leveled the playing field for communication, and it may lessen the significance the five supporting technologies will have on future supply chain communication.

Passing by EDI

EDI was developed more than 25 years ago to remove some of the human interaction needed to exchange data. It eliminated paperwork and handled a large volume of trans-actions, and its rigid communications standards ensured that there were no errors in the transactions. It was the only game in town for companies wanting to streamline communications with a select few suppliers.

Times have changed since EDI was introduced and EDI is becoming viewed as a lumbering, expensive dinosaur in today's world of high-speed, cheap Internet connections and Web-based applications. EDI's requirements for rigid standards don't meet today's need for flexibility, and its transactions move across a proprietary value-added network (VAN). VANs are costly, ranging from $15 to $38 per megabyte (MB) of data transferred, which costs a company like Federated Stores $20 million annually.

For some time now, companies have been looking for ways to circumvent the cost of EDI. Some companies have implemented EDI-to-Web applications in which Web servers receive standard EDI formats from companies with EDI capabilities and convert or map them into data that is stored in a database. Some of the e-business technologies that can be used to enhance EDI and even replace it are

- XML—An easy-to-write, cross-platform software language that enables designers to create their own customized tags to provide functionality not available with HTML. XML is expected to extend the ability of users with workstations to become part of the trading community through its Web-based form applications.
- Internet-based business communication/Web-form EDI—Enables smaller businesses to communicate with larger trading partners through Web site access. A user goes to a Web site, pulls up the appropriate form, and enters data. Some systems verify the data against a database.
- Extranets and intranets—Private and semi-private Web sites for companies and their commerce partners. These are discussed later in this chapter.
- Business-centric portals – Portals that centralize an industry. Many business-centric portals are procurement-related.
- FTP (file transfer protocol)—A protocol that is gaining in popularity with small companies for point-to-point EDI delivery. There are companies that provide specific connections for firms that wish to send EDI data from a translator to a designated server, completely bypassing a VAN mailbox.
- E-mail—Used to send unstructured material.
- Application-to-application—Also known as buy-side e-commerce for business-to-business (B2B) applications. This is discussed in the next section.
- Application service providers (ASPs)—Another type of Internet service. ASPs lease server space to companies so they may host software applications without buying a server (which is a high-dollar item). Often, ASPs will lease applications to companies. Software and hardware maintenance are the ASP's responsibility.

Other communications methods will replace EDI eventually, but it will take many years. One common interim scenario is using EDI for business partner communications and the Web for consumer-based communication. This is not the communications necessary for Supply Chain Excellence, however. Communications for excellence are seamless, and occur over the Internet and on the Web, not in various forms for various functions.

Business Applications

Applications vendors and developers have been using the Web to create enhanced relationships between supply chain partners for some time now. They have concluded that user interfaces for systems will be browser-based and that client/server applications will be replaced with thin clients, multi-tier applications, XML, and enterprise-strength Java. To these ends, they are developing Web-based applications that exploit the separation of business data and databases from the user, manage various forms of messaging, and break up data into small chunks for better security. These applications are called business applications. The task they are most likely to accomplish is to allow one company's business systems to communicate directly with another company's business systems over the Web.

Business applications are also being developed to meet the needs created by a shift from client/server computing to multi-tier computing. Multi-tier computing, also referred to as three-tier computing, is computing on at least three tiers: client, application server, and back-end legacy systems. Business applications reside on the middle tier (the application server) and are therefore called middleware. Middleware applications are used to connect and integrate data from back-end, legacy systems and present them in a format that can be accessed by any client. The client can be anything from a workstation to a palm-sized computer.

Examples of Web-based business applications include those used to design extranets, supply chain planning and execution systems, spreadsheet macro languages, packaged simulation tools, enterprise information systems that support key business processes and house enterprise data, and data warehousing systems. These applications rely on the "write once, use everywhere" principle of the Java language. They are non-proprietary, which means they may be used by different operating systems (e.g., Unix, Windows, Solaris) and clients across enterprises.

The most common use of middleware is to connect ERP systems to the supply chain. ERP has been very useful to organizations, but it does little to remove the boundaries between supply chain partners. Because many corporations have invested significant amounts of money in their ERP systems, they are reluctant to dispense with them altogether.

Middleware not only allows communication between ERP and peripheral applications, but it also integrates them. Proponents of Collaborative Planning, Forecasting, and Replenishment would argue that this is a waste of time, but to companies who have been satisfied with ERP, integration represents middle ground between "business as usual" and huge investments in new communications systems.

Supply chain communications are most often between existing systems rather than new systems. Business applications and their Web-based interfaces and languages allow communications between all kinds of systems. Therefore, business applications are critical components of supply chain communications.

Extranets

The use of extranets for supply chain communications continues to grow. An extranet is an intranet that is partially accessible to authorized outsiders through an address on a Web browser. A valid username and password provide access to the extranet and that identity determines which parts of it may be viewed.

Extranets resulted from the revolution in business communication created by the Web. Previously, companies designed one system for communicating inside the business and another for use outside. The Web changed that whole communications paradigm.

Extranets are most likely to be used as Web sites where suppliers and buyers can exchange materials and services privately. These are often known as private trading exchanges. Public trading exchanges also exist, but they are not extranets, nor have they been very successful.

Extranets have the following characteristics:

- Information is stored across the expanse of the communication network rather than in separate data repositories.
- Those sending and receiving information are as close to one another as they can be, with neither electronic nor human filters.
- Individuals can act on information as soon as it is available.

These are similar to the characteristics of communications for Supply Chain Excellence. Those wishing to achieve Supply Chain Excellence, therefore, should embrace extranets. They should include them in their communications strategies, because they reduce expenses and cycle times-two key requirements for Supply Chain Excellence.

Collaborative Planning, Forecasting, and Replenishment

The Voluntary Interindustry Commerce Standards (VICS) Association developed Collaborative Planning, Forecasting, and Replenishment (CPFR) to meet what many companies and communicators felt was a deficiency in ERP systems, which integrate some functions but do not address the entire supply chain. CPFR allows collaborative processes across the supply chain that are:

- Open, yet allow secure communications
- Flexible across industries
- Extensible to all supply chain processes
- Able to support a broad set of requirements (new data types, interoperability with different database management systems, etc.)

This is a radical departure from traditional planning, forecasting, and replenishment. Usually, computer software is used to compare historical trends and generate a forecast. Anyone with additional information revises the statistical forecast in hopes of improving accuracy.

CPFR specifies software tools for synchronizing and exchanging data with the intention of integrating systems and providing support for collaborative forecasting and replenishment processes, with the goal of increasing sales and reducing inventory investments and cycle time while facilitating agility and demand planning. It involves collaboration among all the partners who affect the value of the end product. Customers contribute to the generation of numbers and participate in other parts of the process. It changes relationships from buyer/seller to partner/partner as customers' purchase orders become collaborative forecasts and replenishment orders.

Technically, CPFR specifications, recommendations, and discussions of technical implementation criteria fall into in four areas:

- Data format standards—These must be selected from the ANSI X12 Electronic Data Interchange (EDI) standard and the Standard Interchange Language (SIL) standard.
- Transport/network protocol guidelines—The transmission of messages between CPFR trading partners must be based on data transport (e.g., FTP) protocols and underlying network protocols (e.g., TCP/IP).
- Security considerations—Partners must select techniques for authentication, encryption, non-repudiation, and origin of CPFR messages.
- Application/middleware—Partners must agree on alternatives for the location, coordination, and management of the data processing elements (servers, agents, and other components) that make up a CPFR implementation.

All CPFR implementations must use approved data formats.

The key requirements for CPFR are real-time, global, secure, and simultaneous communication. Real-time information is a requirement because outdated information has no

The Value of CPFR —TrueValue and Delta Faucet

As the result of a merger in 1998, TrueValue, a subsidiary of the TrueServ Corporation, realized that it needed to improve product line logistics among its 7,600 independently owned retail units, 1,700 stocking vendors, and 14 DCs. It had also identified cash-flow pressures, dissatisfied customers and owners, and millions of dollars in excess inventory. The Illinois-based company also determined that antiquated inventory systems, overlapping networks, and outdated technology had caused these problems. To eliminate the problems and make needed improvements, the company embarked on a collaborative commerce program that allows the company to work with trading partners to establish a single, shared demand forecast.

In 2001, TrueValue approached Delta Faucet, one of its major trading partners, concerning participation in a CPFR initiative. Following discussions, the two companies established a front-end agreement. This included a review of baseline performance metrics, such as security views, mutual goals, review periods, and execution resources. With these goals established, supplier training commenced and included defining best practices, functional training, certification, and a review of TrueValue policies. TrueValue and Delta Faucet then established a setup audit, a review of the existing business plan, and live execution. This took about a week. Following live execution, a series of scorecard reviews and additional category planning integration occurred.

In addition to a rapid implementation time, TrueValue has noted several benefits, including improved service levels, promotional analysis, and forecast accuracy. It has also noted increased promotional service levels and reduced inventory across the distribution network. Finally, the retailer has increased gross sales by 10 percent to 20 percent above previous levels for vendors participating in the program. — About.com, February 18, 2002

value and creates both a delay as partners wait for reorder point replenishment and a buildup of inventory. Global communication is necessary because CPFR is a worldwide phenomenon. Secure communication is critical for establishing trust between multiple supply chain partners. Simultaneous communication is a requirement because the information must be shared between all interested parties at the same time. Otherwise, the supply chain remains time-phased and linear, rather than nimble and responsive.

Beware of the Bells and Whistles

The various information systems and data formats introduced in this chapter will help your supply chain create the communications necessary for achieving Collaboration, the fourth level of Supply Chain Excellence, which eventually leads to Levels 5 and 6, Synthesis and

Velocity. But while you pursue various networking and collaborative tools, you should remember an important point. You can link as many suppliers, retailers, and customers as you want on the Web, but if you don't communicate properly, your partnerships and alliances will fail.

Having systems with all the cool bells and whistles is not what's important. What is critical is that your supply chain use communications to create the supply chain partnerships described in Chapter 13, agility, and synchronization. If you use your systems and formats to that end, everyone along your supply chain can achieve Supply Chain Excellence.

Conclusion

This chapter and the seven before it have discussed the eight core competencies necessary for achieving Supply Chain Excellence: Change, Peak-to-Peak Performance, Total Operations, Customer Satisfaction, Manufacturing Synthesis, Distribution Synthesis, Partnerships, and Communications. Once these competencies are mastered, you have the tools and skill sets necessary for Supply Chain Excellence. The final part of this book addresses how to use them.

15

The Technology for Supply Chain Excellence

"Technology primarily deserves the credit for having the financial courage, the ingenuity, and the driving energy to see to it that so-called 'pure knowledge' is in fact brought to the practical service of man."

— Warren Weaver

Supply Chain Excellence is all about using partnerships and communication to synthesize the supply chain. It is also all about removing boundaries at every level in the supply chain. I hit upon this realization while working with a client several years back. An analysis of this client's supply chain resulted in a series of opportunities for improvement. As we drilled down into these opportunities, it became clear that before we could pursue Supply Chain Excellence with this client, we needed to address the company's own links because there were boundaries between its plants that had to be removed. Then, as we began to look inside the plants, we saw an even more basic problem: substantial boundaries between the departments. We saw that eliminating those boundaries had to occur before we could address the boundaries on the plant-to-plant level.

Working with this client allowed me to see that if an organization and its supply chain want to achieve Supply Chain Excellence, it has to start at the lowest level and move up. Supply Chain Excellence is the result of moving up the six levels in sequence and removing boundaries as you go. This cannot be accomplished without technology—IT, the Internet, the World Wide Web, and various forms of business software. Technology is the enabler in the process of achieving Supply Chain Excellence. Therefore, any supply chain technology architecture implemented must assist supply chains in this quest. This can be accomplished by looking at each level critically, starting with Level 1, and considering the technology

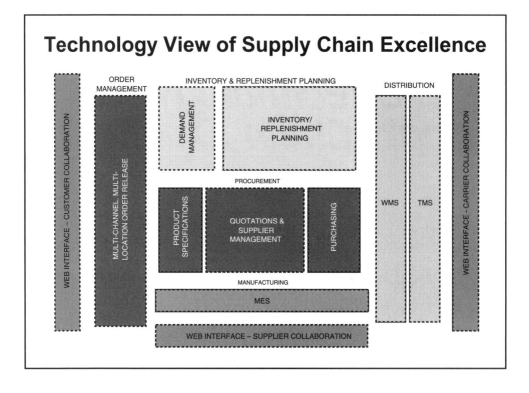

needed to go to the next level. This is not to be construed as the technology to achieve the level, but technology that sets the stage for achieving each level above until Level 6 is reached.

Today, companies are pursuing technology, but usually as an end unto itself or with the expectations that if the technology systems go in, then all the problems will be fixed. Consequently, the same problems are popping up as those that arose with previous technology systems (MRP, ERP, DRP, and others.) For technology to enable Supply Chain Excellence, operational practices must be changed and improved. Silos must be broken down. Links in the chain must pursue working together rather than simply talking about it. Good examples are visibility and collaboration. Many companies have put these systems in, but very few are really doing collaboration. They use the systems for visibility into the links of the supply chain, but then each link uses this information independently to try to optimize itself. The links are not synthesizing or synchronizing the supply chain.

Because of this trend, I would like to emphasize again that acquiring the technology necessary to achieve one of the levels is not going to lead to Supply Chain Excellence.

You must put technology in place with an eye to being able to use that technology to move to the next level. For example, it is not enough for your company to install technology to help you achieve Visibility; you must install the systems, software, and applications that not only allow Visibility, but also use the Visibility to achieve Collaboration. Acquiring and installing the technology for Supply Chain Excellence is like achieving Supply Chain Excellence itself—it requires using one level as the stepping stone to the next.

In the previous chapter, I discussed the various technology backbones required for the communications necessary for Supply Chain Excellence. This chapter introduces the functions that the systems needed for Supply Chain Excellence must provide, then it follows with a basic overview of the technology architectures necessary for reaching each level and moving to the next.

System Functions for Supply Chain Excellence

The functions that systems must provide for Supply Chain Excellence can be categorized as follows:

1. ERP—core financial systems—core backbone systems—financial management
   - General ledger
   - Budget management
   - Human resources
2. Marketing systems
3. Sales systems—customer relationship management systems
   - Sales force automation
   - Call center management
   - Field service
4. Planning systems
   - Forecasting
   - Demand planning
   - Event planning
   - Constraint-based optimization
   - Manufacturing master scheduling
   - Inventory optimization
5. Procurement systems
   - Sourcing
   - Purchasing—purchase order systems

- Contracts
- Supplier scheduling
- Replenishment systems
- Total cost management
- Marketplace exchanges

6. Manufacturing planning and execution systems
   - MRP
   - Shop floor control, scheduling and management
   - Bill of materials
   - Work in process inventory
   - Process automation and control
   - Quality
   - Automated data capture
   - Cost management

7. Fulfillment
   - Order management systems
     - Order entry
     - Pricing structure
     - Inventory management and allocation
     - Order release management
   - WMS
   - LMS
   - TMS
   - Routing systems
   - Shipping systems—Manifesting systems (Bills of lading systems, especially package manifesting systems)
   - Slotting system
   - Yard management system
   - Network analysis software

8. Store systems (retail only)
   - Point of sale (POS)
   - Store inventory systems
   - Merchandising

9. Supply Chain metrics and reporting systems
   - Financial

- Sales
- Marketing
- Manufacturing
- Fulfillment
- Customer service

The following sections discuss these functions in the context of the Six Levels of Supply Chain Excellence.

The Technology for Level 1—Business as Usual

To move up from Level 1, companies need technology solutions that allow the company to begin seeing itself as one entity instead of loosely connected departments trying to outdo one another. The first step should be integrating accounting practices with a core financials package that handles accounts payable, accounts receivable, and general ledger. Core financials systems offer benefits in key areas, including:

- Financial management
- General ledger
- Budget management
- Human resources

More sophisticated packages include budgeting, payroll, electronic banking and payment of invoices, and other functions. The package a company should choose depends on the company's size, its type of business, and the types, volumes, and complexity of its transactions.

Integrating core financials acclimates a Level 1 company to the notion of integration. It helps the company understand what can be accomplished by breaking out of the silos of individual departments and divisions and how necessary this transition is if they wish to remain in business. It also prepares them for the technology used at the next level.

The Technology for Level 2—Link Excellence

The technology necessary for achieving Link Excellence has a profound effect on achieving Supply Chain Excellence. Therefore, it is critical that technology at the link level not only perform the tasks it was designed to do, but also be flexible, scalable, reliable, and modular. The focus should be company-wide execution, with some emphasis on planning at the inventory level. Software applications for order management, transportation management, warehouse management, manufacturing execution (if the business is both a manufacturer and a distributor), demand planning/forecasting, parcel manifesting and e-procurement are required, as are an updated Web site and simulation software (for a multiple-site distribution network). It is important to take a look at each in the context of Link Excellence.

Order Management Systems

Order management systems (OMSs) manage order entry, pricing structure, prioritization, and inventory allocation, and they release orders for fulfillment. In other words, they streamline several different link functions and encourage cooperation between the individual departments involved in the order-taking and order-fulfilling processes. The OMSs necessary for Link Excellence accept orders (electronically, through a Web interface, or by manual entry) and manage them for standard or valid customized products, using the product configuration tool to select alternative parts. They also target and plan telesales activities because they have excellent tools for customizing the desired information on screen. Other features include smart order entry with online information for immediate response to any inquiries; continuous and detailed customer and product information; online shortage product allocation based on customer priority or fair share handling; "non-stocked" order processing and effortless drop shipments.

Transportation Management Systems

Transportation management systems (TMSs) provide modules for transportation services procurement, short-term transportation planning and optimization, and transportation plans execution. Many TMSs focus on inbound optimization, and shippers have more options than before to assist them in the planning and execution of a comprehensive inbound freight management program. They also feature continuous analysis and collaboration.

Transportation services procurement applications can facilitate the request-for-proposal (RFP) process, perform spot procurement of transportation services, and provide strategic procurement, whereby shippers establish long-term contracts with carriers. Transportation planning and optimization solutions address strategic, tactical and operational challenges that can constrain the execution process. Transportation execution solutions handle all activities involved in shipping a product from origin to destination.

In a TMS, integration between shippers, carriers, and other trading partners is accomplished either directly (e.g., one-to-one system integration) or via a collaborative logistics network. Shippers can use the latter to access most (if not all) trading partners via a single integration point. They may also use it to plan and execute shipments jointly. When the correct system is implemented successfully, it can reduce transportation costs, inventory, and customer order cycle time. This, in turn, increases customer satisfaction, a key element in Link Excellence and Supply Chain Excellence.

Warehouse Management Systems

Warehouse Management Systems (WMSs) that meet the requirements of Link Excellence are software applications that facilitate the receipt, movement, control, and fulfillment of orders received from an order management system. These systems direct and control, in real-time, all activities and resources in the warehouse, including inventory, people and equipment from receiving to shipping. A WMS selects space for inventory storage, determines the most efficient sequence of picking and which individuals and equipment will be involved, and identifies and manages cost-effective packing and shipping.

The correct WMS for Link Excellence creates shorter order cycle times and increased order fill rates. Inventory accuracy of over 99.9 percent, reduced labor requirements within the warehouse, and a significant improvement in customer satisfaction levels are among the other benefits.

Manufacturing Execution Systems

Manufacturing execution systems (MESs) are critical to achieving Link Excellence for manufacturers. These systems dynamically control highly automated manufacturing processes with receipts or bills of materials to drive highly automated production processes through to completion. Their capabilities include allocating, reserving, scheduling and dispatching resources. Typically, they are used in conjunction with a supervisory control and data acquisition (SCADA) system to drive controls at the shop-floor level. SCADA systems are flexible, extensible human-machine interface (HMI) applications that ease integration, monitoring and control of complex systems and may be used in the warehouse or on the manufacturing floor. They integrate proprietary machine controllers from various manufacturers into a cohesive functional manufacturing or distribution solution.

With dynamic control, an MES can handle changing conditions such as re-routing work or resetting priorities to eliminate machine downtime. They can also factor inventory into the work plan and readjust production as necessary. This is critical when a company must handle conflicting customer demands for finished goods.

The benefits of these systems are lower manufacturing costs, less inventory, and improved order planning and scheduling. They reduce lead-times more than 20 percent and condense manufacturing cycle times by 35 percent. They also create a decline in work-in-process (WIP) levels of 30 percent, a big driver of Link Excellence.

Demand Planning/Forecasting Systems

Demand Planning/Forecasting Systems are necessary for achieving Link Excellence, because they integrate both historical and current customer demand with inventory supply processes, such as manufacturing, distribution, or procurement. They can reconcile demand history, existing customer orders, point of sale (POS) data, market forecasts, and other information. This creates a clear, comprehensive overview of demand by item, location, customer and/or group that may be used by everyone in the link to determine demand patterns and ensure an executable plan that has considered all current operational constraints.

Demand Planning/Forecasting Systems increase revenue by reducing lost sales and reduce costs by lowering inventory while at the same time increasing customer satisfaction levels of the most profitable customers. They support accurate merchandise and manu-facturing planning processes and provide more accurate forecasts for new products. Also, these systems easily adapt to organizational needs through forecasts at multiple product and location levels.

Parcel Manifesting

Parcel manifest systems should be part of the tools portfolio for achieving Link Excel-lence. They facilitate shopping for parcel carrier rates, update rate tables from those carriers, electronically pass shipment information to selected carriers, and print packing labels that are compliant with each carrier's shipping requirements. The benefits of these software applications include carrier compliance labeling, operational efficiency for distribution, and freight capture for customer billing. Most parcel manifest systems are integrated with a WMS application.

Procurement Systems

Procurement systems come in a variety of flavors and offer various levels of functionality. The most basic systems generate transactions or purchase orders and send them to sup-pliers automatically. These are helpful, but alone they cannot help a company achieve Link Excellence. Instead, companies should look at systems that offer a Total Cost Management solution that can be used to capture and manage spending and provide streamlined pro-curement operations within the organization and throughout the supply chain.

The systems best suited to companies seeking Link Excellence are e-procurement systems that use refined business processes and supplier relationships supported by technology to automate these processes, eliminate the paper, reduce errors and ultimately cut the administrative costs. They handle blanket orders, sourcing contracts, releases against an order and enforcing full or partial receipts. Other functionality may also be part of the system. They may also include a catalog automation system, an application that captures a company's catalog information from an inventory management application or legacy system and presents it via a Web-based interface. Automated sourcing, smoother workflow, the elimination of paper, enforced negotiated pricing, approved suppliers, and the significant reduction of maverick buying (purchases made without following standard company procedure) are among the benefits of e-procurement.

Additional Applications for Link Excellence

Depending on the complexity of the company or the systems already in place, companies may want to consider additional planning and management applications, including

- Inventory planning systems. These systems optimize stocking levels, order quantities, reorder methods, and activity-based costing (ABC) analysis for each SKU and warehouse location. They can create a 10 percent to 40 percent reduction in inventory.
- Automatic data capture systems. These systems are used with legacy and ERP systems that have not developed sophisticated automatic data capture technology. They streamline manufacturing and warehousing transactions for complex systems and give companies the flexibility to model data capture after their process requirements instead of conforming to system requirements.
- Enterprise asset management systems. These systems control all physical assets from a cost, life expectancy, and preventive and predictive maintenance standpoint. They can reduce overall downtime by 10 percent to 20 percent and thus increase capacity.
- Route management systems. These systems are used for a business that requires direct store delivery, like Coca-Cola. They optimize the delivery route based upon a variety of factors, including driving time, average unload time, and amount of product needed at each store for that delivery period.

Retail businesses should also explore two other applications: retail merchandising systems and retail price management systems. Retailers can use retail merchandising systems to determine what products to put in each store, how much of each SKU, and how to display it for the best sales. They feature perpetual inventory and merchandising on a scalable backbone; local market targeting and tailored presentation; optimizing price points, markdown management and competitive pricing and predictions of the impact of promotions on inventory, margin and revenues.

Retail price management systems manage multiple retail channel pricing structures, such as retail store, Web site, and re-sellers. In other words, a retailer can use the software for effectively managing a large number of SKUs, thereby ensuring the correct price of each item at the store, catalog, or Web site.

Setting Your Sites on Link Excellence

In addition to the systems we've just discussed, Link Excellence requires a Web site with e-commerce functions. The Web site may be hosted or in-house and offer simple e-commerce functions for browsing a catalog and ordering products. It must be integrated with a back-end inventory system so that the status of stock is visible.

Simulation software is fast becoming a preferred solution over network modeling software due to its flexibility in handling fluctuation in demand patterns. Simulation software runs multiple variations and flexible "what-if" scenarios using inherent probabilities, then returns several options for solutions. Simulation can be used successfully in a logistics network design project as well as for determining a lowest-cost sourcing choice for new product introductions. However, no system, Web site, or simulation can help a company achieve Link Excellence without the IT knowledge and expertise to determine what systems from which vendors will work with one another and how and where they should be integrated or installed.

Companies must not only be aware of what technology is offered at the Link Excellence level but must make sure their decisions are for the long-term. A thorough study of organizational processes and activities and a strategic master plan for achieving Link Excellence are musts before an organization embarks on any IT purchases. Once a company has the technology in place for Link Excellence and it is running smoothly, it can begin to consider the technology it needs to achieve Visibility.

The Technology for Level 3—Visibility

Through Visibility, organizations come to understand their roles in a supply chain and are aware of the other links. Sharing information so that trading partners understand and have time to react to events such as order status updates, promotions, manufacturing schedules, advanced shipment notices and shipment-tracking numbers minimizes surprises. This requires commitment to the technology that makes internal information available not only within the company, but also to select supply chain partners.

The ideal solution for Visibility with an eye to Collaboration is an Enterprise Application Integration (EAI) suite to capture all relevant data in disparate applications and databases and tie them together so they can be presented in a common format. Though this is a huge undertaking, it implements the infrastructure required to support the other Visibility technologies—an executive information system (EIS) and supply chain event management (SCEM).

An EIS (also called a dashboard) pulls together all key performance indicators (KPIs) and presents them via a browser in near-real-time, giving company management the information it needs to make decisions quickly and effectively. SCEM provides trading partners (suppliers and customers) critical event notifications on order status, schedule changes, invoices, shipment tracking and many other areas to give them the most time possible to react to changes that occur.

Internally, visibility and communication are critical to keeping everyone pushing the company in the right direction. Due to security concerns that exist around air travel, streaming media, such as video conferencing, video training courses, video-on-demand and other media rich services should be considered as the ideal solution for internal communications. These are critical to doing business globally.

Visibility also requires specific types of software applications. These applications execute, manage and plan with a focus on supply chain procurement, inventory replenishment and customer relationships, as well as integrate and interact seamlessly with the systems in place for Link Excellence. They are discussed below.

Procurement Applications

Several variations of procurement technology are used at the Visibility level to create an intranet e-procurement hub. Public and private procurement exchanges are one example of this technology. These usually focus within a vertical sector to optimize buying clout and expert knowledge of specific commodity groups. They are found in the various industries, including chemicals; industrial supplies; maintenance, repair and operating (MRO) supplies; aerospace, and so forth. Initially, companies should use these exchanges to make purchases via the Internet with an open line of credit or procurement card. More sophisticated users should then integrate this functionality into an intranet hub for all employees with pre-approved suppliers and negotiated pricing contracts based on the company's consolidated spend.

Another procurement and sourcing application is configuration management software. Its purpose is to eliminate incompatible component choices when building a product specification. These applications are most likely to be found in complex electronics industries that are likely to use an e-commerce site to select, for example, a model number of a product such as a handheld RF gun and then choose a monochrome or color screen. Based on the product selected, the software drives the selection of processor speed and memory, operating system and wireless protocol requirements among other options and ensures that customers order valid configurations of products.

Replenishment Planning Applications

Replenishment planning applications consider the effects of inventory investment, service levels and current orders and commitments, seamlessly matching profitability to customer response. They can easily manage high volumes of SKU/location combinations, and they have strong distribution resource planning (DRP) features that provide multilevel insight into demand and inventory. Perhaps even more important, these DRP capabilities have been especially designed to enhance widespread collaboration, even in a complex distribution network.

Replenishment planning views inventory from a number of perspectives, including actual demand data, future distribution needs, and replenishment commitments. It is also exception driven so that planners can quickly focus only on those situations where supply and demand are out of balance. As a result, planners can spend their time making informed decisions about resource allocation, expediting orders and enhancing customer satisfaction rather than tending to routine replenishment orders that replenishment planning software can handle automatically.

Replenishment planning anticipates and averts problems such as stock-outs and outdated inventory. Minimizing obsolescence, the solution presents planners with economically sound options and pleased customers. Other benefits include quicker response to market demand, timely orders and deliveries, and improved inventory turns.

Customer Relationship Management Applications

Customer relationship management applications traditionally include three primary modules: sales force automation (SFA), call center management, and field service. Sales force automation tracks all opportunities from prospecting to closure, with extensive visibility into the pipeline. Call center management automates either phone or Web-based order entry, product support call-center activities that flow back into product development, and text-based instant messaging with customers who need live product support. Field Service modules remove paper from the warranty support process, provide extensive Web-based status updates to customers and plan and coordinate service technicians' site repairs. Some allow Web-based appointment scheduling.

Other Software and Applications for Achieving Visibility

The applications discussed above are instrumental for Visibility. However, certain auxiliary systems and applications can smooth planning, scheduling and event management processes so that they are transparent and seamless. These include:

- Advanced planning and scheduling systems. Advanced planning and scheduling (APS) software creates accurate, effective plans that meet service targets, as well as true least-cost, least-change, inventory limits and other related goals. These applications speed long-range capacity planning, tactical master production schedules, and even work center schedules at individual plants. From a "big picture" perspective, APS software can look across all facilities to attain schedules for a single production line and accurate models of the production environment. It coordinates multiple component manufacturing plants into a single assembly plant so that they work much like the automotive assembly process.

- Event planning applications. Event planning (sometimes called promotion planning) simulates the sales impact of alternative marketing programs. Neural-network models analyze multiple elements, such as price discounts, coupons, advertising and product placement, to predict consumer behavior. They feature forecasting models for thoroughly and accurately planning, tracking and analyzing the profitability of an entire promotion or the effectiveness of specific promotional features and components. Forecasting models are also incorporated into a live "what-if" environment for testing and evaluation of future promotional plans.

- Labor management systems. Labor management systems (LMS) can set standard times for each discrete task required to receive, put away, pick, replenish, pack and ship product within a warehouse. Interfacing with a WMS, the LMS will calculate a "standard" time for that total task assignment as each worker accepts it. When the workers have completed the task, the system will give them immediate feedback on their performance measured against the standard time. Management can use LMS reports to determine if times need adjustment or if specific workers need further training to improve productivity.

- Inventory slotting system. An inventory slotting system works in conjunction with a WMS to monitor demand continuously at the stock-keeping unit (SKU) and location level, and it adjusts the amount of product "slotted" in each location. Inventory slotting applications also optimize the slot each product should occupy to minimize travel distance and labor. Well-integrated systems create location moves within the WMS to drive proper slotting.

- Yard management systems. Yard management systems (YMSs) are designed for large distribution centers (DCs) that manage multiple carriers and a large number of trucks each day. The YMS schedules carrier arrival and departure times for each dock door at receiving and shipping. A YMS will manage staged trailers that are pre-loaded prior to carrier arrival to minimize wait times at the DC. At the same time, they measure compliance for any contractual issues.

- Automated/integrated reverse logistics. Automated/integrated reverse logistics applications are typically found in catalog or Web merchant businesses and automate the product returns process and capture real-time data that can be put back into the marketing and sales cycle. They not only control the product direction, but also the carton, pallet and shipment builds for efficient processing at the product destination. These applications provide a uniform system for effective communication that decreases the chances of human error. Exception handling takes care of special requests based on criteria such as volume or serial number. RMA (return materials authorization) tracking, disposition by inspection and condition processing will quickly and efficiently return products to market, route them for "rebox," or direct them to their ultimate disposition.

With the addition of an automated customs settlement system, these applications, systems, and software create the visibility the supply chain needs so it can move to the fourth level, Collaboration.

The Technology for Level 4—Collaboration

The focus of the technology at Level 4 is supply chain systems integration (as opposed to internal systems integration) with a view to sharing knowledge, building strong relationships with supply chain partners so they may work together to reduce costs, reducing cycle time, increasing responsiveness, synchronizing supply with demand, and making continuous improvements. For example, a Web site for a company at Level 4 integrates critical front-end and back-office data systems to provide Tier 1 customers with a complete picture of where the supply chain stands.

Critical to the success of collaboration technology is a data warehouse. Data warehouses consolidate huge amounts of data from multiple systems into a repository for searching. With this repository, supply chains can develop market intelligence based on trends that emerge from analyzing data such as information about purchases. The applications that mine this data and accomplish the system integration necessary for collaboration are discussed in the sections that follow.

Integrated Transportation Management Applications

Integrated transportation management applications aggregate and analyze pre-shipment data in real-time. They collect purchase orders, sales orders, and ship notices and compare the data before the shipment leaves the dock. They also analyze logistics data and alert users to exceptions, such as mismatched quantities, products, or destinations. Through these activities, this software:

- Eliminates missed shipments
- Eliminates shipment discrepancies
- Minimizes shipment mistakes
- Minimizes the need for reverse logistics
- Increases delivery reliability
- Increases the efficiency of inbound and outbound logistics operations

In a net marketplace, this technology will allow global logistics planning and optimization.

Inter-Enterprise Application Integration Applications

Inter-enterprise application integration (IAI) applications are another example of middle-ware. Unlike enterprise application integration (EAI) applications, which integrate applications within the enterprise, these applications integrate applications between two or more different enterprises. Typically, they integrate CRM, e-commerce, and EAI applications and they should have the following characteristics:

- B2B e-commerce emphasis
- Architecturally superior integration skills
- Embedded performance management agents
- Rapid but structured time-to-market approach (e.g., fixed price, fixed time)
- Post-implementation application management (i.e., continuous transformation).

IAI also speeds the exchange of data between enterprise databases and internet-based users via portable languages and protocols, such as XML, EnterpriseJavaBeans (EJBs), and Java.

Supply Planning/Product Life Cycle Management

Supply planning/product life cycle management balances resource allocation and customer service levels against the operational constraints of the entire supply chain. These applications identify where to make or buy products, and they evaluate production, storage and transportation constraints on profits. The result is an optimal plan based on dynamic, real-time sourcing.

Supply planning supports demand tracing as well as multi- and simultaneous-sourcing. Real-time alerts allow users to prioritize and manage the supply chain at optimal efficiency. Also included in these applications is the intelligence to incorporate various fulfillment-planning models such as available-to-promise (ATP), capable-to-promise (CTP), and profitable-to-promise (PTP).

ATP is the process of systematically looking at current inventory levels and manufacturing orders and determining if and when the order can be shipped. CTP is ATP plus looking at inbound inventory and forecasted orders to determine when the order can be shipped. PTP looks at all of the above plus the customer placing the order and prioritizes the order based on how profitable that customer is. For example, a supplier may have the inventory to fill an order, but it may tell the company that placed the order that it is going to take longer depending on how much money the supplier has made on previous sales to that company.

Other Applications for Collaboration

Other applications for Collaboration are available and should be included in the design of Level 4 technology. They are:

- Collaborative manufacturing systems. Similar to APS systems, collaborative manufacturing systems operate at a more granular level. After a schedule is complete and is being executed, these applications allow immediate reaction, collaboration, and resolution of events that take place across multiple-site manufacturing processes.
- Demand collaboration. Demand collaboration applications provide the flexible framework that accelerates visibility and velocity across the supply chain so that partners can work seamlessly across disparate applications and organizations. Demand collaboration

automates and manages multi-tiered collaboration between suppliers, manufacturers, distributors, and retailers. It collectively improves sales and order forecasting, planning, exception and alert notification, promotion planning, business trend analysis, and more.

- Sales and operations planning. Manufacturers and independent distributors or distributors and remote sales forces can use sales and operations planning applications to manage development of a forecast remotely. The forecast can be broken out on the basis of sales person, region, account, etc. Users can input details, and the application then summarizes them into a corporate-level sales plan that can then be used to drive manufacturing planning and scheduling.

- Catalog API for supply chain partners. API is the abbreviation for application program interface. It is a set of routines, protocols, and tools for building software applications. A catalog API for supply chain partners integrates the electronic catalogs of approved vendors into an intranet site that supply chain partners can use to make purchases.

- Supplier relationship management applications. Supplier relationship management (SRM) applications are similar to CRM. The difference is that SRM typically takes into account relationship planning, contracts with suppliers, and alternate suppliers for items, while measuring how well a supplier meets performance levels. They also find specific performance problems with suppliers and monitor improvements automatically.

- Fulfillment collaborator. A fulfillment collaboration application extends collaboration to trading partners that manage transportation and distribution centers. Fulfillment collaboration synchronizes vital functions throughout all fulfillment operations. Companies can share real-time order-fulfillment communications with customers, suppliers, and carriers, thereby creating improvements in key performance measures, such as on-time and complete-order fill rates and eliminating traditional efficiency bottlenecks. Fulfillment collaboration includes tools that manage communications related to customer orders, freight shipments, suppliers' products, and more from an inventory and shipping perspective.

Once the technology necessary for collaboration is up and running, the next step is to use it for the pursuit of synthesis—Level 5 of Supply Chain Excellence.

The Technology for Level 5—Synthesis
It is from synthesis that true Supply Chain Excellence is achieved because Synthesis enables a supply chain to reach unparalleled levels of performance.

At Level 5, all goals for technology excellence have been reached. The company's leaders have a strategy is in place to keep the supply chain's leading edge through systems review and evaluation. They continually update a prioritized list to target system upgrades, replacements, and improvements, and this drives the capital budget. Non-core competencies are in the process of being outsourced.

Unlike at the other levels, Level 5 operates as if it only had one platform. This can be accomplished in two ways: integrating everything into one platform (Windows, Unix, Linux, Netware, Mainframe) or choosing best-of-breed applications and integrating the various platforms and applications. Pockets of other operating systems that provide a tactical/competitive advantage may remain, but these are the exception rather than the rule.

At Level 5, the technology for the lower levels is in place, live, and operating smoothly because they are the foundation for the technology that will synthesize the supply chain. In fact, they simplify synthesis because they have been installed with that in mind. For example, in Web sites operating at this level, all transactions are integrated internally and externally into core business processes and access is open to all supply chain partners. The core financials packages include letter of credit, bank draft, and automatic invoice payment applications to streamline some of the complex issues in international trade.

The Level 4 data warehouse is mined by data-mining software that aggregates the multiple sources of data, which can then be used to determine the exact buying patterns of customers (retail or otherwise). For example, retailers can learn what time of day or year customers buy more products. This type of data mining allows very targeted promotions to drive business even higher.

Level 5 software must help smooth the supply chain into an entity without silos, links, or boundaries. This may be accomplished with intelligent agent technology and other agility and synchronization applications. Intelligent agent technology assigns rules-based intelligence to every order, component, or item in a manufacturing or distribution environment. The agents decide what actions to take with other external systems to manage execution orders developed from planning systems. If a high-priority order arrived on the last day of the month, this system would simultaneously optimize the delivery date and ensure that the change affected as little as possible. If a greater impact is unavoidable, these applications would notify the planner and customer.

The applications best able to synchronize the supply chain into an agile entity are:

- Collaborative issue resolution. This application works in conjunction with SRM software to manage issues with suppliers, 3PL providers, and other partners, and then track them

Collaborative Product Design: *Anchor Group*

A consumer products manufacturer, the Anchor Group (Sacramento, CA) produces apparel for a number of widely known international retailers from its Sacramento and Hermosillo, Mexico, plants. Anchor uses a product design collaboration application that integrates with an ERP application for both internal and external product design. Anchor decided to implement the application because the various processes that made up product flow were loosely defined—often only in the mind of an individual. These processes needed to be formalized into organized process workflow so they would not be lost.

Now, Anchor's art department receives sample specs from a customer and initiates a workflow sample order, which consists of entering customer and program information and then checking the specs into the electronic vault. Once the order is complete, it is routed back to the customer for approval. After it is approved, the customer sends the purchase order via EDI/XML, and the order is processed for production. The application provides a central repository for all engineering and art collaboration, routing communications and tasks internally.

— Supply Chain Systems, May 2002

through to resolution. Collaborative issue resolution also monitors execution systems to ensure any contractual performance requirements are not missed.

- Workflow automation. Workflow automation computerizes a defined series of tasks within a supply chain to produce a specified outcome. Workflow automation software ensures that those responsible for the next process task are notified and receive the information they need to execute their step in the process.
- Collaborative product design and engineering. With these applications, engineers at multiple sites can collaborate on design and engineering to cut time to market drastically. A manufacturer can also use it with several Tier 1 components suppliers.

These applications will ensure the continuous flow of information and set the stage for achieving Velocity, the sixth level of Supply Chain Excellence.

Level 6—Velocity

Since Velocity is synthesis at the speed of light, the focus of the technology for Level 6 is speeding synthesis and keeping it nimble. Most of the technology that can accomplish this is already in place by the time a supply chain is ready to move to Level 6. Therefore, the supply chain simply needs to upgrade its Web sites and refine its intelligent agent technology.

Level 6 Web sites integrate all internal and external transactions into core business processes. The external transactions include those with Tier 2 and 3 customers and suppliers, as well as Tier 1 partners. Supply chain partners use them to manage and configure their own accounts as required.

Conclusion

Supply Chain Excellence technology creates simultaneous, instantaneous, and multi-directional communication so that all supply chain partners work together at the same time and in real time. The technology necessary for each level is put in place with all this in mind. It eliminates inventory buffers and accelerates the flow of cash. It promotes dynamic planning, which replaces the outdated practices of long-term forecasting. It makes strategic information available to all partners so that all have contact with the customer and are aware of changing needs and trends. They can then respond in unison.

The key to success is to make sure that all the technology necessary for each level is in place and running smoothly before moving to the next level. If companies and supply chains try to skip a level or skimp on technology, it will not help them in their quest for Supply Chain Excellence.

16

Globalization for Supply Chain Excellence

"In today's world, where businesses are global and people are refining things down to the last cent of efficiency, you can't be all things to all people."

— Steve Rogel, Chairman, President and CEO, Weyerhaueser Company

Strong and agile supply chains that cross borders are meant to shake things up, to make life more difficult for competitors. Creating such supply chains is possible through globalization, which is the act of integrating and coordinating economic activities worldwide. The Battle of Hastings in 1066 may have been the first time that a notion like globalization met head-on with the traditional thinking about boundaries. In this renowned historical battle, William, Duke of Normandy, invaded Great Britain and defeated the Saxons led by Harold, King of England. William, known as "the Conqueror" for his success, took over the British monarchy. On that October day in the 11th century, Great Britain moved closer to Europe than it had ever been. No channels of water could completely separate it from the continent ever again. Information was being shared, alliances were being forged, political systems re-envisioned, and commerce between the nations of Europe strengthened. In effect, William was adding links to his supply chain beyond the rigid geographic boundaries of France to derive more competitive advantage.

Of course, globalization is better achieved these days with "point and click" than by "invade and massacre." IT, deregulation and privatization in most countries, a global financial system, and a worldwide market economy have made modern-day supply chain globalization possible. Why is this good news? It's because a global supply chain is the only kind of supply chain that can synchronize supply with demand, become agile, and achieve Supply Chain Excellence, and those actions pack far-reaching benefits. For example, globalization allows a supply chain to handle shorter product life cycles. It offers organizations the largest possible market in which to recoup their development and procurement costs quickly. By going global, supply chains quickly gain the flexibility, modularity, and adaptability required to achieve Supply Chain Excellence because a supply chain that operates in several countries can take advantage of different economic cycles and seasons.

Some other benefits of globalization are:

- Economies of scale and scope are extended because of the larger market globalization creates.
- Outsourcing is maximized because globalization creates a wider selection field.
- Customer satisfaction is increased as companies can offer localized service from closer facilities, increasing responsiveness.
- Productivity is accelerated as supply chains exploit the various advantages of different countries.
- Global inflation is stemmed by worldwide competition.
- Innovation is encouraged by open economies and worldwide competition.
- Export-related jobs are increased, and they often pay more than other jobs.
- Low interest rates are created by free-flowing capital worldwide.

Globalization has come a long way since William, and it carries different requirements. Successful globalization depends heavily on pushing aside boundaries to reach foreign markets and to receive their goods and services in return. This chapter discusses the trade agreements and regulations that drive the global economy, explains how information systems and technology support the global economy, then puts both in the context of Supply Chain Excellence.

Reaching Out

In a global economy, reaching full economic potential means reaching out to other countries. The late Ron Brown, U.S. Secretary of Commerce, once said, "We know free trade means progress for all people, and that with open markets come open systems." For much of the mid-20th century, American protectionist policies ran counter to what Brown believed, and that had a cost. For example, after the U.S. hesitated to penetrate the Latin American markets, Europeans took a substantial interest in the Caribbean, capitalizing on its consumer, labor, and resource pools.

Fortunately, in the last two decades, trade agreements have been established that encourage open markets. At the same time, new plans and laws were being made and existing laws were being broadly enhanced to encourage closeness in partnerships and alliances, new options like virtual business, and outreaches to neighbors beyond geographic borders.

One such plan is the Global Information Infrastructure (GII), whose principles are that the private sector should spearhead expansion of the Internet and e-commerce within a simple, consistent legal environment and with few government restrictions. An example of broad enhancements to existing laws is the changes that have been suggested in the Uniform Commercial Code (UCC), which has been adopted by every state except Louisiana, which enhances commerce through the unification of substantive commercial laws. The UCC was formulated under the assumption that all trading would be on paper, so parts of it failed to address an electronic environment. Companies considering either a traditional EDI/VAN package or a more innovative EDI/Internet connection were lost on some issues. So, in response to these needs, some basic changes were made to the entire UCC and the changes passed on to the states for implementation. "Record" replaced "writing," and "authentication" replaced "signature." The UCC also introduces the "electronic/intelligent agent," which is a computer program used by a party to communicate electronically without review by an individual. Choosing an electronic agent binds an organization to the actions of the electronic agent.

There are several variations on the issue of how electronic commerce will accommodate the requirements for signatures and verification that everyone understood for paper commerce. There are numerous proposed laws at both the federal and state levels in the U.S., and similar issues are constantly evolving within other nations and internationally. Industry groups make proposals, and legislation and regulations by governments will influence e-commerce and, by association, global trade. Just one example is the Electronic Transactions Act proposed in the U.S. by the National Conference of Commissioners on Uniform State Laws (NCCUSL). Its language would recognize electronic records and agreements as substitutes for paper, assure that signature requirements can be met through electronic means, and modify the rules of contract law as they apply to transmission and receipt of communications. Some states have adopted the language.

The International Chamber of Commerce has a program called General Usage for International Digitally Ensured Commerce (GUIDEC). There is a United Nations Commission on International Trade Law (UNCITRAL) model for rules and norms to validate and recognize contracts formed through e-commerce and to support the admission of computer evidence in courts and arbitration proceedings.

The Global Regulatory Environment and Supply Chain Excellence

Reaching beyond the geographic boundaries that separate nations is critical to achieving Supply Chain Excellence. Businesses in Europe welcome and (informally) utilize the supply chain's potential more readily than their American counterparts—and Americans could learn much about trade alliances from them. Europeans then could benefit from American philosophies on information technology. European firms generally perceive replacing IT systems as a huge, costly undertaking—a mentality that runs counter to the U.S. continuous improvement philosophy.

Developing nations like Mexico, Poland, and China embrace foreign investment. These countries, often known for their adaptable, flexible attitudes, offer attractive opportunities in exchange for assistance in improving infrastructure and national welfare. Partnerships and alliances are at the heart of Supply Chain Excellence, and global partnerships that encourage cooperation and collaboration between organizations in different countries are essential in the quest for Supply Chain Excellence. Plans that encourage the use and recognition of electronic signatures and authentication, the acceptance of electronic communications, and the promotion of efficient and effective e-commerce dispute-resolution systems can contribute to global agility and Supply Chain Excellence because these are ways to do business without borders.

Another product of this global regulatory environment that affects Supply Chain Excellence by providing open, timely information is the Trading Partner Agreement (TPA). A TPA is a formal contract that fills in the blanks left by existing contract laws, rules of evidence, and issues of liability. Key elements are a statement of intent, a clarification of liability, security, signatures, and a receipt. The TPA can prevent disagreements and misunderstandings and is an attractive deliverable to offer supply chain partners new to the principles of Supply Chain Excellence. Each should be unique, because each supply chain is unique, and care taken to tailor the agreement to the needs of each supply chain partner.

Information Systems and Technology

Without information systems and technology, borders and boundaries would still define the global economy. The Internet has created a migration from the vertical enterprise of Henry Ford's day to the virtual enterprise. In this world, managing the integration between organizations and those who provide them with competencies outside their core competencies (e.g., manufacturing, logistics, sales, or distribution) requires technologies that can visualize and personalize. These technologies need the ability to identify each unique partner so that various terms and agreements are accessible for transactions over secure lines. These technologies include encryption, authentication, password controls, and firewalls.

The Internet offers these technologies and more. It allows companies to reach into new, global markets and create new ways to serve those markets with:

- Channel management – creating new channels or enhancing existing relationships with channels through better information, speed, and service
- Enhanced collaboration – achieving performance improvement with trading partners through simplified communications
- Market-making – creating new products and services
- Knowledge management – sharing knowledge and techniques across the enterprise and with key trading partners to develop new products and conquer new markets

With these new processes comes a need to manage information, including managing content, knowledge, and innovation, as well as managing partner relationships. These needs have created a new thinking such as

- Thinking in terms of revenue per employee
- Thinking of inventory in terms of days of supply (DOS), i.e., viewing inventory in terms of days and even hours
- Thinking in terms of no days sales outstanding (DSO), where the money from the customer is in the bank before suppliers are paid
- Thinking in terms of negative asset intensity (i.e., no capital investments to create business initiatives)
- Thinking in terms of return on marketing investment
- Thinking terms of agility, i.e., time to market, cycle times, and response times

The new global economic thinking created by the Internet contributes to Supply Chain Excellence in various ways. Projects that seemed impossible before the Internet created global connectivity can now become a reality. For example, the Internet and information technologies can:

- Promote a focus on employees as assets rather than expenses, using their knowledge to gain efficiencies or expand markets as they use the Internet to serve on cross-boundary teams

- Master customer relationship management through technology investments that link companies to the ultimate consumer
- Meld business processes together
- Create a place for the customer in the information infrastructure
- Manage virtual structures and create new financial models for them
- Design new compensation plans for employees
- Create security for safe navigation across Web-based business communities
- Leverage various media to create brand and process recognition

The Internet removes the boundaries that made the above capabilities difficult to achieve in years past. Communications can be sent anywhere in the world in real-time. That is what makes the above list of strategies possible.

Global Strategies

Innovative thinking is necessary to convince your supply chain partners to leave protectionism behind and embrace the concepts of the new world economic order so that they may achieve Supply Chain Excellence and create agile supply chains. Already, creative thinkers in the automotive and electronics industries are developing strategies that may be used to promote these concepts. Not all strategies are similar, but they agree on four principles for promoting global supply chain initiatives:

- Create a global supply chain vision. This vision must motivate employees and trading partners to view the world as their supplier through techniques designed to minimize and eliminate resistance to change, cultural biases, and stereotypes. The two most common techniques are rotating managers on global assignments and communicating to suppliers the need for world-class performance and improvement.
- Organize for global sourcing. This requires a restructuring to provide a cohesive management framework. The restructuring must create global commodity councils, total-cost decision-support systems, global purchasing offices, and global information systems. Global commodity groups facilitate the coordination and integration of different business units. Global cost-decision models are used to develop and share total-cost information associated with different supply options. Global purchasing offices effectively develop global supply knowledge. Global information systems collect information on global supply sources and market trends.

The Cultural Considerations of Globalization

Anyone conducting global business must be aware of cultural differences, especially if that person is selling a product, idea, or alliance. Some of the most important cultural differences to consider are:

- Language. In any global exchange, knowing your trading partner's language improves the quality of the relationship and makes things go more smoothly. This applies even in large global corporations that have made English their official world language.
- Punctuality. In the United States, Northern Europe, and Japan, punctuality is extremely important when transacting business. In other regions (e.g., some Latin, Middle Eastern, and African countries), it does not receive the same importance.
- Exchanging information. In France and some other countries, written information exchanges are preferred to other forms. Other countries, including the U.S. prefer oral communications.
- Decision-making. In certain Latin American, Middle Eastern, and African countries, those at the head of the organization make the decisions and hand them down for implementation with minimal or no discussion. In those cultures, an executive who consults subordinates may be perceived as weak and indecisive. In Japan and South Korea, the opposite holds true. Decisions made by one or a few people, are difficult to implement.
- Motivation. In the United States, emphasizing individual financial rewards usually results in cooperation. In Japan and South Korea, appealing to group welfare works better.
- Authority. In certain Latin American, Middle Eastern, and African countries, an executive's authority derives mostly from family or tribal ties. In the United States, Scandinavia, Germany, and others, it is determined by a person's position in the organization.
- Graft. In the United States, it is illegal to offer inducements to officials of any organization, anywhere in the world. In many other countries, there is a far more relaxed attitude toward such practices. This is an important consideration for American companies competing in foreign markets with non-American companies using such practices, frequently with the help of their governments.

- Configure a supply base. To achieve Supply Chain Excellence, this must be a truly globalized supply base that leverages supplier capabilities all over the world. The suppliers in this base can supply any location worldwide with competitive pricing, quality, delivery, and technology performance.

- Develop supplier capabilities. This is done not by telling a supplier to improve, but actually using a hands-on approach to helping partners achieve performance improvement.

Such strategies have No Boundaries. Thanks to the Internet and real-time communications, the geographic locations of source materials, manufacturing plants, value-added processing, storage, and distribution are irrelevant. The issue becomes elapsed-time-to-market, response to demand-creation, and sustainable value-creation. In other words, the location of an item is less important than knowing when it will be available.

Conclusion

The underlying theme of Supply Chain Excellence is No Boundaries. The global implication of this is enormous. Supply Chain Excellence is not only about No Boundaries between links and partners—it is also about No Boundaries (or borders) between geographic locations. Achieving Supply Chain Excellence requires that we view the world holistically—the best strategy for achieving success and agility in today's global economy.

17

The Supply Chain Excellence Path Forward

"A road to a world with no borders, no boundaries, no flags, no countries"

— Carlos Santana, Grammy Award Winner

The journey to Supply Chain Excellence is the best kind of journey—one that takes you into the future. Although we live in the present, we must always be thinking about the future to achieve Supply Chain Excellence. This does not refer only to the near future, but to the distant future as well. It is the same as Peak-to-Peak Performance: We should not be looking only at the next peak—we should be looking at the next next peak and the peak after that one and the peak after that.

Those who wish to achieve Supply Chain Excellence cannot rely on the methods of the past for success. Supply Chain Excellence means breaking new ground and forging a path forward to success with agility and No Boundaries. This is not to say that you can make up Supply Chain Excellence up as you go along. You must have a definite plan that includes the Six Levels of Supply Chain Excellence and the strategies necessary for moving from level to level. Otherwise, you'll wander aimlessly and get lost. It is likely, however, that your plan will put you on a path that has not been trod before.

Those of you who have read all the way through the book may be a bit puzzled at this point because you are remembering that achieving Supply Chain Excellence is a continuous improvement process. As such, a plan for achieving it will be revisited often. So isn't that a path backward? Let me put your mind at rest: It is not. Each time a process is improved, it is not the same process—it is only the same type of process. You may be

Aligning Supply Chain and Corporate Strategies: Southwest Airlines

Aligning a supply chain strategy and its associated metrics with corporate strategy is critical when devising a plan for achieving Supply Chain Excellence. In the 1970s, Southwest Airlines capitalized on a niche market—short-haul flights between major cities in Texas. From Southwest's perspective, its main competitors were cars, not other airlines, because the time it took to drive from city to city was sometimes shorter than the time spent flying. Southwest's corporate strategy was to be the fastest mode of transportation between cities and to compete with automobiles in real cost and opportunity cost. The airline aligned its supply chain accordingly by making several tradeoffs to achieve breakthrough performance in cycle time, or turnaround time as it's called in the airline industry. These included no assigned seating, no inter-airline baggage or ticketing, and standardized airplanes for quick maintenance between stops. Southwest also made tradeoffs to create a cost structure that enabled it to compete with driving.

— *ASCET*, May 5, 2002

laying down the same type of stone or brick that you've laid in a path before, but now it is in a new place.

A plan for a Supply Chain Excellence has the following steps:

- Establish a Supply Chain Excellence Steering Team
- Conduct a supply chain assessment
- Develop a business plan
- Conduct Customer and Supplier Roundtables
- Conduct Leadership Roundtables
- Define a Supply Chain Excellence Vision and what your Evidence of Success will be
- Define prioritized Supply Chain Excellence opportunities for improvement
- Establish a Supply Chain Excellence Communication Team
- Establish Supply Chain Excellence Improvement Teams
- Implement the Supply Chain Excellence Improvement Teams' recommendations
- Assess the Evidence of Success
- Define new prioritized opportunities for improvement.

This chapter will examine these steps— with the exception of the supply chain assessment, which is the subject of the next chapter—defining them where necessary and using examples where appropriate, so that you may use them in your own plan for an Supply Chain Excellence path forward.

Establish a Supply Chain Excellence Steering Team

The Supply Chain Excellence Steering Team will define the direction the supply chain will be taking to achieve agility and Supply Chain Excellence. This team's members should come from the top level of each supply chain partner's organization, ideally, the top leaders. Because the Steering Team will be responsible for driving the supply chain toward Supply Chain Excellence, its members must have a clear understanding of Supply Chain Excellence, knowledge of the role(s) of each partner in the supply chain, good insight and foresight, and healthy imaginations.

The purpose of the Supply Chain Excellence Steering Team is to establish, communicate, and maintain focus on Supply Chain Excellence and to develop the business plan, vision, and evidence of success for it. Supply Chain Excellence Steering Team members should individually and collectively demonstrate this focus. They must also demonstrate a united commitment to Business Process Continuous Improvement (BPCI) and the process of Revolution. Their first action should be to develop a charter. This charter should include the team's scope, the problem-solving and decision-making processes for the team, quantitative measures for the team and its deadlines, team resources, team budget, constraints, and authority. All members should be aligned and should understand the team charter, as it will serve as a guiding document for the team. The team should hold regular business meetings and periodic checks to make sure that commitment to the charter and Supply Chain Excellence continues to run high.

Conduct a Supply Chain Assessment

A Supply Chain assessment is a critical examination of where a supply chain is, as well as a measure of its health. A successful method for conducting the assessment is detailed in the next chapter. This assessment will play a key role in the prioritization step.

Develop a Business Plan

The Supply Chain Excellence Steering Team is responsible for developing a business plan for Supply Chain Excellence. This should be a multi-year, macro-level, agile business plan that will serve as the requirements definition for the future of the supply chain. Therefore, it should be a set of goals and performance measures to assure that all partners have a common view of the path forward. This will help the Steering Team and other leaders stay focused on Supply Chain Excellence. It also will help prepare them for changes in the supply chain.

Conduct Customer and Supplier Roundtables

The term "roundtable" has several definitions. The definition that best suits Supply Chain Excellence is "a meeting of peers for discussion and exchange of views." Customer and Supplier Roundtables should include representatives from suppliers all along the supply chain, as well as the ultimate consumer. The purpose of the roundtables is to provide a facilitated opportunity for suppliers and customers to share ideas about products and markets interactively, query existing beliefs, and uncover new opinions.

The information collected from a Customer and Supplier Roundtable provides unique input into the development of a strategic plan for achieving Supply Chain Excellence. The relationships fostered between customers and suppliers are invaluable. For example, participants gain a clearer view of the complexity of supply chain relationships and become more confident as together they develop solutions from the roundtable questioning process.

Supply chain partners should conduct Customer and Supplier Roundtables regularly so that supply chain members and the Steering Team are aware of changes in the supply chain. They also need to be continuous. Each roundtable prepares follow-up questions to elicit even deeper understanding of the future.

Conduct Leadership Roundtables

Leadership Roundtables operate on the premise of intellectual power. When used with the process of strategic planning, they can be highly successful tools. However, like other means of gathering data and assessing it so that conclusions may be drawn, a Leadership Roundtable requires a high degree of skill, experience, and technical competence. A successful roundtable uncovers data that will benefit all planning processes, including the one for the multi-year business plan.

The participants in Leadership Roundtables should have an interest in and a knowledge of a given part of the supply chain. They should also be leaders in their respective organizations. To capitalize on Leadership Roundtable results, a consistent methodology must be applied:

- The purpose must be clearly defined and understood
- Participants must be present and ready to interact openly

- A neutral setting and atmosphere of amnesty must exist
- A carefully designed set of questions must be administered by a facilitator, who provides unbiased input to the strategic planning team

Define Vision and Evidence of Success

A vision for Supply Chain Excellence is not the doubletalk and doublethink so prevalent in American business today. Instead, it is the type of vision I defined in my book *Revolution*: "A description of where you are headed." The vision for Supply Chain Excellence should be stated so that the present is described as a past condition of the future, not as a future condition of the past. It should express optimism, hope, excellence, ideals, and possibilities for your supply chain for tomorrow. An example of a vision for the automotive industry might be, "To be the world's best and most agile automotive supply chain by creating true partnerships with suppliers and customers, continuously improving customer satisfaction, using the best and most effective methods of technology communication, and harnessing the energy of change."

My recommendation for any Steering Team defining its vision of Supply Chain Excellence is to create a robust Model of Success. As Warren Bennis, the author of *On Becoming a Leader*, said, "Action without vision is stumbling in the dark and vision without action is poverty-stricken poetry." In reality, a vision is only part of an entire Model of Success, which comprises:

- Vision—A description of where you are headed
- Mission—How to accomplish the Vision
- Requirements of Success—The science of your business (or in the case of Supply Chain Excellence, the science of your supply chain)
- Guiding Principles—The values to practice while pursuing the vision
- Evidence of Success—Measurable results that will demonstrate when an organization (or supply chain) is moving toward the vision

To define the Evidence of Success, those who defined the first four parts of the Model of Success must define the organizational entity to be measured, the perspective of measurement, and the performance to be measured. In the case of Supply Chain Excellence, the organizational entity is the supply chain. The perspective for measurement could be partners, customers, and suppliers. The performance to be measured could be:

Defining Opportunities for Improvement: *Juniper Networks*

Juniper Networks provides edge and core routing solutions for government agencies, research and educational facilities, enterprise businesses and top network service providers worldwide. Juniper outsources every aspect of manufacturing, from prototyping through mass production. In late 2000, the company realized that, to avoid costly surprises and make its manufacturing supply chain more stable, it would have to implement a system to give it better visibility into and control over its extended supply chain network.

Since that time, Juniper Networks has implemented a broad supply chain solution that allows it to see deep inside the activities of its supply chain partners. This solution also helps Juniper Networks identify changes and issues before they become problems, to analyze the potential impact of those changes, and to act decisively to ensure the best possible outcome.

How does it do this? By providing the company with desktop access to real-time information about key supply chain indicators and giving it the opportunity and the means for taking action on important changes. All individuals in the organization can immediately access the information necessary for making decisions that best serve customers and ensure the highest quality and performance. Juniper Networks is also able to take guidance and operational governance procedures set by the organization and incorporate them into that action. Because of these benefits, the solution is now a critical application for continuous measurement of supply chain performance and execution at Juniper Networks. — Juniper Networks Success Story, Valdero Corp., 2002

- Supply chain health
- Supply chain effectiveness
- Supply chain efficiency
- Supply chain quality
- Supply chain partnerships
- Supply chain communications
- Supply chain financials.

It will be up to all supply chain partners to determine how these should be measured. One method would be to model the Evidence of Success along the lines of the supply chain assessment.

Define Prioritized Opportunities for Improvement

The supply chain assessment is a very useful tool in defining opportunities for improvement in the process of achieving Supply Chain Excellence. For example, a client of ours has evaluated each of the core requirements for Supply Chain Excellence based on its current operations. Its total evaluation reveals that target areas for improvement are customer satisfaction and manufacturing synthesis. As a result of that, it knows that the overall health of the supply chain is poor as well. These target areas were determined when each criterion in the audit was investigated.

After determining the core competencies of Supply Chain Excellence, the organization focuses its continuous improvement efforts on the two areas listed above, using a Communication Team and Improvement Teams.

Establish a Communication Team

The responsibility of a Supply Chain Excellence Communication Team is to ensure and assure that everyone in the supply chain has a clear understanding of the Model of Success for Supply Chain Excellence, the status of teams, and the status of the supply chain. Like all teams, it should have a charter with the components I described in the section on the Steering Team. All teams involved in the process of achieving Supply Chain Excellence need charters.

The Communication Team has many tools at its disposal for conveying these messages, but it must also keep in mind that these communications will travel across many organizations all over the world, so they must be familiar with electronic forms of communication. I also recommend that the Communication Team schedule regular Communication Forums. These forums are essential to ensuring alignment, understanding, and celebration. Such a forum should consist of a review of the Model of Success for Supply Chain Excellence and team or partner presentations that cover the status of their role in Supply Chain Excellence, their questions about Supply Chain Excellence, and challenges they may be facing. Since supply chain partners most likely will be in different areas across the globe, it might be wise to investigate electronic ways of conducting these. No Boundaries to communication should separate them.

Establish Improvement Teams

The Improvement Teams are where the Supply Chain Excellence process resides. For supply chain partners to achieve Supply Chain Excellence, they must create and charter many Improvement Teams all along the supply chain. These teams then must focus on incremental and continuous improvement in the areas defined in the process of prioritizing opportunities for improvement. Some of these teams will be cross-functional: They will address a specific improvement opportunity with representatives from across the supply chain. Others may be functional and address improvements in the organization of a specific partner.

The members of the Improvement Teams should be from broad cross-sections of the upply chain and should have demonstrated in the past that they are capable of achieving continuous improvements, breakthroughs, and innovation to enhance performance. The scope of each Improvement Team charter should be consistent with the knowledge of the members on the team and of sufficient focus to allow the team to achieve real performance improvements. It is critical that these teams meet as often as necessary so that they may develop specific recommendations and plans of action to achieve peak performance in the areas that need improvement.

Implement Recommendations of the Improvement Teams

The Improvement Teams' recommendations are to be shared with the Supply Chain Excellence Steering Team for review and approval. Once the Steering Team approves the recommendations, they should be implemented. Communicating the approved recommendations then becomes the task of the Communication Team. The Steering Team should remain committed to implementing the recommendations throughout the implementation process.

Assess Evidence of Success

Those involved with implementing the Improvement Team recommendations and the Supply Chain Excellence Steering Team should maintain an ongoing record that tracks performance against the defined Evidence of Success. The record should be reviewed periodically to prioritize the next opportunities for improvement. The Communication Team should disseminate information about ongoing continuous improvements throughout the supply chain.

Define New Prioritized Opportunities for Improvement

Based on another supply chain assessment conducted after the Evidence of Success that shows that performance has improved, the Steering Team should prioritize the opportunities for the next iteration of the Supply Chain Excellence process. This is continuous improvement in action. Supply chain partners working toward the goal of Supply Chain Excellence should never stop looking for ways to improve. They must lay down the same types of stones or bricks in the path again and again if they wish to keep moving forward.

Conclusion

Successful improvement implementations may not remain successful. Supply Chain Excellence is a dynamic process; like the river with which I like to compare it, it is always moving. That means supply chain members should move with it, and continuous improvement efforts are the best way to keep up with the motion. Never-ending peak-to-peak evolution is the process that will provide your supply chain with the competitive advantage required to achieve sustained and agile Supply Chain Excellence.

18

Assessing Supply Chain Performance

"True balance requires assigning realistic performance expectations to each of our roles."

— Melinda M. Marshall

To achieve Supply Chain Excellence, gain agility, and win competitive advantage in the supply chain vs. supply chain wars, a supply chain must be synchronized and performing at its best. If it isn't, anything it has gained will be short-lived. Yet, many companies are not aware of how their supply chains are performing or even that they are portions of a supply chain. This is not a disaster for the chains, however—it is a repairable problem. A strategic assessment methodology that uses specific assessment criteria based on the Six Levels of Supply Chain Excellence can help partners determine how their supply chain is performing and plot a course for improvement. This chapter presents the methodology for assessing your supply chain, then offers a detailed discussion of the criteria and what characterizes each of the six levels.

It all depends on a solid understanding of the Six Levels of Supply Chain Excellence explained in Chapter 3. With that structure as a guide, a hard, honest look at each link in the supply chain will reveal what level each link has attained and what boundaries need to be cleared away so the supply chain can climb toward Velocity.

Supply Chain Strategic Assessment Methodology

Unused information is value-less. It is what you do with information that makes the difference. The supply chain assessment methodology is an assembly manual for what otherwise could be a big box of unmarked parts. It explains how to use the component information to build a continuous improvement process for the supply chain.

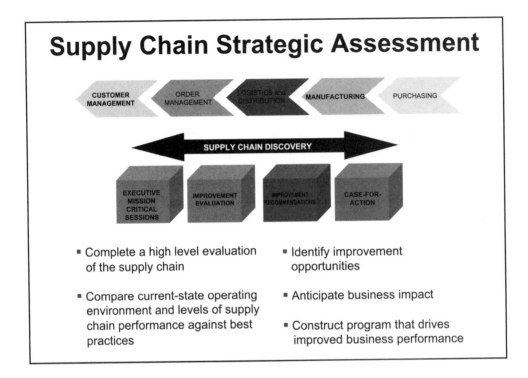

The Supply Chain Strategic Assessment Methodology has seven steps:

1. Map the current state of high-level business processes. Document information flows, business rules, and so on. Determine if they meet business and mission-critical goals. Are they automated? Could they be outsourced if conditions warranted that? How well are they measured? When you have those answers, you'll know better where there are functional gaps, where lack of automation is slowing down your supply chain, and where there are organizational issues. This will help you identify both tactical and strategic improvement opportunities.

2. Drill down into the business processes. Here, you are looking to see how the processes are linked-and to make sure they are linked-and to find out what information is flowing and what the processes need. Develop a detailed process flow to show the connections so everyone in the supply chain understands the relationships. This step includes under-standing and documenting your supply chain's KPIs, assessing the state of information technology, and assuring there is 360-degree feedback among executives and business process owners.

3. With the more detailed knowledge of the process linkages, develop a current-state map of the supply chain that shows external supply chain relationships-where there are links and where there are gaps.

4. Evaluate the data collected in Step 2 and arrive at conclusions about the processes in your supply chain. You may conclude, for example, that there are processes that do not have ownership, processes that are not well-documented, processes that do not map well to your company's or supply chain's goals and mission, and processes that are not automated.

5. Develop supply chain process recommendations. This is where you draw the map of how processes should work, based on what you have learned in your examination.

6. Recommend the actions necessary to get to where you need to be. Devise high-level implementation plans for those actions. Determine the savings that the recommendations can produce, and calculate the ROI. Assess the availability of internal resources versus what will need to be brought in to accomplish the goals.

7. Develop a detailed implementation plan and set the priorities for the steps in it so you can begin the path forward.

With this methodology, the partners in the supply chain can compare their current-state operating environment and levels of supply chain performance against best practices. The exercises carried out and the maps produced, in turn, allow you to identify improvement opportunities, anticipate business impacts, and construct a process that drives improved business performance.

The Assessment Criteria: The Six Levels of Supply Chain Excellence

The assessment will be most effective when everyone involved is, as the old saying goes, on the same page. That is why it is critical to understand the Six Levels of Supply Chain Excellence. They offer a yardstick by which to measure the components in a supply chain: enabling technologies, supply chain planning, communications, synthesis, warehousing, logistics, manufacturing, organizational excellence, maintenance, and quality. Each component has distinguishing characteristics at each of the six levels. Measuring these components will help you identify your supply chain's level and its constituents partners' levels.

The sections that follow discuss each component and its characteristics at each level.

Enabling Technologies

Enabling technologies include IT infrastructure and solutions, RF interfaces with mobile assets, Web enablement, and common databases/elements with a single version of the information.

Enabling technology at Level 1 consists of legacy and homegrown systems. Islands of technology have been acquired and installed as a reaction to specific situations. Duplicate entry and databases are rampant. At Level 2, a link's transportation management system (TMS), warehouse management system (WMS), and order management system (OMS) have been recently upgraded to industry standards and information visibility is internal. At Level 3, systems are integrated within and across the organization. The TMS, WMS, OMS, and supply chain operations systems link to key partners to share information. Duplicate entry is limited.

Information concerning events and plans is freely shared among first-tier partners at Level 4. Information has been integrated into each organization's execution and planning systems. Basic Enterprise Information Systems (EIS) are present. At Level 5, first-tier partners collaborate. A robust EIS is automating key performance indicators (KPIs). Level 6 enabling technologies are characterized by synthesis with a forum for continuously improving timing, quality, and quantity among multiple tiers of channel partners.

Supply Chain Planning

The goals of the supply chain planning component include strategic sourcing relationships; standardization, design, and specification management; planning, forecasting, and replenishment; reverse logistics; electronic marketplaces; and synchronization of supply and demand.

At Level 1, sourcing decisions are based almost exclusively on low price. At Level 2, cost of acquisition replaces price to include transportation, quality, and flexibility. At Level 3, partnerships are formed with key suppliers, and the partners share current and historical demand information. At Level 4, major suppliers participate in product design and planning activities, including demand planning and supply chain planning. Information is visible to all, and transactions are electronic and Web-enabled. Consideration is given to better synchronizing supply with demand.

Interactive design and/or replenishment over multiple levels of the supply chain characterize Level 5, where Supply Chain Excellence Steering and Supply Chain Excellence Improvement teams facilitate continuous improvement and systems are put in place to

UDDI Compliance

Critical to achieving visibility is a strategy for becoming compliant with Universal Description, Discovery, and Integration (UDDI). Major application providers, such as Ariba, IBM, and Microsoft, have announced that they will lead in the creation of a new industry template and registry for the digital marketplace. The purpose of this free, publicly hosted application is to facilitate the transfer of information between any two companies on how to do business with one another over the Web.

Adopting the model of a Domain Name Service (DNS) registry, UDDI will utilize platform-independent XML and Simple Object Access Protocol (SOAP) technology to create virtual Yellow Pages for Internet-enabled businesses. In addition to providing information on a company's products, services, contact information, and the like, UDDI will define what type of e-business platforms a company is using, thereby smoothing the process for electronically conducting business. The UDDI initiative will also create a registry domain on the Internet. This will allow businesses to register themselves and will provide the host domain for searching for a given product or service.

The first version of the UDDI template will be structured on a three-tier architecture defined as white pages, yellow pages, and green pages. Within this template, a company can describe its business and the methods by which it conducts e-commerce. Subsequent versions will provide a much richer descriptive context. In version 2, UDDI will layer pages of information for additional security. Consequently, businesses will be able to make some information public, such as their trading addresses while other information, such as volume discounts, can be limited to qualified users who have identified themselves and met appropriate screening criteria. Version 3 will gain custom taxonomies and workflow rules.

synchronize supply with demand. When the Supply Chain Excellence teams move online and the lead-time of synchronization is short, then supply is at Level 6.

Communications

The communications component comprises links or flow; information integration with other supply chain links; and inventory and cycle time strategies.

At Level 1, companies are interacting with suppliers via fax, phone, and mail. Information is not integrated. At Level 2, they use a limited number of EDI and XML-based transactions. Duplicate information entry is frequent. Level 3 has them exchanging EDI and XML messages for major transactions and events. They use sourcing exchanges occasionally. At Level 4, first-tier partners are exchanging forecasts, marketing plans, and production schedules. The partners are also developing private and public exchanges.

When first-tier partners and other prominent supply chain constituents are being advised of changes in the partners' schedules and all is synchronized, the chain has reached Level 5. At Level 6, response to supply chain events across multiple tiers of partners drives the changing of schedules.

Synthesis

The synthesis component has an inter-link planning process, event management and tracking, a performance measurement scorecard that crosses multiple links, and partnerships for continuous improvement.

When this component is at Level 1, a budget determines planning and is the measure of performance. At Level 2, the enterprise may be sharing annual or quarterly requirements, and there may be some information integration. The enterprise is maintaining metrics for on-time deliveries as well as quality and the completeness of orders.

The sharing is bumped up a notch when synthesis moves to Level 3. Suppliers and organizations share detailed forecasts. All partners in the link maintain enterprise-wide scorecards, and there is full integration of internal information. Also, APS systems are in place, and the enterprises comply with Universal Description, Discovery, and Integration (UDDI).

At Level 4, partner input helps create forecasts and plans. Scorecards are the tools for supply chain improvements. At Level 5, supply chain partners are building and updating forecasts jointly, and a continuous improvement effort includes scorecard review. When scorecards, forecasts, and plans are shared beyond adjacent links in the supply chain, the synthesis component is at Level 6.

Warehousing

The warehousing component has intra- and inter-facility integration and it employs technology such as WMS, RF communications, auto ID, crossdocking, and order and service customization. Performance metrics are in place, and the emphasis is design, functionality, and flexibility.

At Level 1, the systems are legacy and home-grown, with no integration. Current operational needs drive the acquisition of warehousing technology. At Level 2, the warehousing component's systems may be partially integrated with order and transportation systems. The warehouse may also have some connectivity with suppliers and customers.

Full integration with other enterprise systems is the hallmark of warehousing at Level 3. There is also connectivity with major customers and suppliers. At Level 4, the supply chain partners are fully sharing inventory and shipping information and schedules. The characteristics of Level 5 warehousing are postponement and product completion just prior to shipping. It is also possible to see virtual warehousing in which links are bypassed in response to customer needs and true synchronization. When that virtual warehousing is a full reality, the warehousing component has reached Level 6.

Logistics

The goals of the logistics component are network rationalization and optimization; TMS, RF, crossdocking, and inbound/outbound consolidation; communication interfaces between links; and outsourcing strategies. Emphasis is on design, functionality, and flexibility.

At Level 1, the distribution network and inventory networks have evolved in response to sales pressure. These networks are not integrated with other functions. At Level 2, distribution networks have been internally rationalized and internal systems are integrated. There may be some connectivity with other partners, and the enterprise has some core carriers. Outsourcing is ad-hoc. At Level 3, the logistics component has continuous network optimization. Its systems are fully integrated with other enterprise systems and are connected to major customers, carriers, and suppliers. Vehicle and inventory tracking is in place, and the logistics function has outsourced non-core functions.

When the outsourcing of non-core functions becomes strategic and there is complete event management and control of global shipments, then the logistics component has reached Level 4. At Level 5, an automated reaction to unplanned events and messaging to first-tier partners, along with full outsourcing of non-core functions, characterize logistics. At Level 6, the logistics component has full flexibility. This is accomplished through IT integration and the outsourcing of variable functions.

Manufacturing

The goal for this component is agile, flexible, modular, upgradable, adaptable, and scalable manufacturing. Lead-time reduction is critical, as is reducing set-up and changeover time. Manufacturing manages constraints and bottlenecks, and it balances operations. It employs planning, execution, and shop-floor technology for continuous material flow.

At Level 1, the manufacturing component is a mixture of traditional processes with limited technology, partnerships, and integration. When it begins to have effective manufacturing processes and IT systems and communications and when link measures are optimized, then it has reached Level 2. Level 3 manufacturing is characterized by fully flexible and modular processes, effective partnerships, seamless communication, and link continuous improvement.

At Level 4, technology and integration cross the links, and manufacturing has true partnerships and a continuous improvement process for the supply chain. Level 5 is achieved when processes are customer-focused, real-time process and information integration is in place, and the continuous improvement process is highly developed across the supply chain. Manufacturing at Level 6 features ever-increasing levels of supply chain speed and responsiveness to customer needs across broader reaches of the supply chain.

Organizational Excellence

Organizational excellence means having inter- and intra-organization accountability, teaming processes, and incentive and reward structures. Costs and benefits from supply chain improvements are shared.

Level 1 organizational excellence is, in a sense, paradoxical because all performance measures are independent. The same may be said for Level 2 organizational excellence, where the basis for the reward structure is silo performance and teaming is largely inside silos, although some cross-functional teaming may be present. At Level 3, the reward structure is based on the company's performance, and cross-functional team structures are prevalent. At Level 4, the company's teaming is cross-functional and inter-organizational, and the focus of rewards and incentives is shifting to the supply chain.

By the time organizational excellence reaches Level 5, a cross-organization process for continuous improvement is in place. Rewards are based on supply chain performance, and the supply chain shares gains and pains. Organizational excellence has reached Level 6 when the partners begin to share the benefits from supply chain improvements equitably, and incentives and rewards are aligned across organizations.

Maintenance

The maintenance component ideal is maintainability, reliability, and asset uptime; increased capacity and throughput; computerized maintenance and management systems (CMMS), preventive maintenance and predictive maintenance; planning and scheduling for a proactive strategy; spares and MRO materials management; craft skills for achieving core management; and a metric for validating a profit-centered strategy. Maintenance at Level 1 is reactive, with a firefighting approach. It is very costly, and the organization views it as

Six Sigma: A Facilities Management Example

Six Sigma is a highly disciplined, project-based methodology that can help companies focus on developing and delivering near-perfect products and services. Six Sigma is based on the idea that, rather than wasting time and money fixing products that come out wrong and dealing with the cost of returns and dissatisfied customers that result, companies should have a goal of achieving "zero defects" or as close to zero as they can get.

In statistics, the Greek letter sigma indicates how far a process has deviated from perfection. In the manufacturing sector, a process achieves Six Sigma quality if it produces no more than 3.4 defects per million opportunities. The idea of Six Sigma is to measure the number of defects in a process, then figure out ways to eliminate those defects.

Now, Six Sigma methods are being applied to any type of organization that wishes to improve its business. Call centers, hospitals, and even juvenile-detention halls are improving some aspects of their operations with Six Sigma implementations. Those considering applying Six Sigma to businesses should consider the answers to the following questions:

- Who are your customers?
- What are their requirements?
- What are the correct metrics?
- How do you measure these requirements?
- How do you improve your processes?

You should also drill down into your processes to see what is causing defects and create a pareto diagram of them. Then, you can focus on the major issues. — Optimizemag.com, May 2002

a function that does not contribute to profit. At Level 2, preventive and predictive maintenance are in place, and there is condition-based monitoring. At Level 3, maintenance has CMMS for improved information, performance reporting, and the enhancement of best practices. When the maintenance function begins cooperative planning with operations and has an internal customer focus, it is at Level 4. Level 5 is characterized by increased certainty of asset uptime, full integration with operations, and a contribution to profit. At Level 6, maintenance has an increased service level and more productive response and execution rates.

Quality

The quality component includes process vs. inspection, vendor certification, accountability, and product design.

Quality at Level 1 features ad-hoc, reactive improvements based on customer issues and concerns. At Level 2, the organization has continuous quality improvement programs within each facility and silo. Level 3 quality is characterized by enforced quality standards from suppliers to eliminate in-plant inspections; proactive feedback to channel partners; and Six Sigma and Total Quality Management (TQM) processes that cross enterprise boundaries.

At Level 4, vendors are participating in the process of designing quality aspects into components and materials for downstream benefits. At Level 5, vendors and customers work together to design quality into components and final products. Quality at Level 6 means that continuous improvement activities are crossing multiple supply chain levels.

Once you understand how each of the preceding components works in the supply chain and you can recognize the characteristics that signal the levels the various components have reached, it is time to use the information. The way to do it is through the Strategic Supply Chain Assessment Methodology.

Success Requires Collaboration

Lest anyone think I do not understand how big an undertaking a supply chain assessment is, let me be very clear. The entire exercise can go nowhere unless the partners in the supply chain can find the will and trust to collaborate in carrying it out. That may be a very big step for some supply chains, a smaller one for others if they are already working up the six levels. It is, however, a deal-killer step. Unless partners can collaborate to find out how they can make their supply chain better, they are doomed to link excellence—at best—and another supply chain is going to eat their lunch sooner or later.

You may be saying, "But I thought Collaboration was Level 4—two-thirds of the way to the top?" Yes, it is the same word, but here partners are asking one another to collaborate only on an assessment. In the best of all worlds, they may find from their assessment that they have achieved Visibility and are ready to try to step up to full supply chain collaboration. In most cases, they will be trying just to agree that they want to do what it takes to find out how they're doing. It may be a tough sell.

Before you embark on an assessment, look inward at your company and ask two key questions:

- How willing is your company to collaborate?
- How willing are the companies in your supply chain to collaborate?

If you poll your company and the others, the answers may surprise you. Many companies are resistant to Collaboration for various reasons, including:

- Short-term financial focus
- Inability to agree on how to share the costs of implementation
- Inability to agree on how to share the savings
- Concerns over visibility and sharing of sensitive information
- Fear of weakened negotiating stance
- Fear that collaboration creates commitments
- History and culture of adversarial relationships
- Links with competing supply chains.

You overcome these obstacles by going beyond willingness and intention and reaching commitment. Collaboration requires discarding the traditional relationships between organizations. Instead, focus on the opportunity for additional contribution to the growth and profitability of the supply chain. This applies to both a customer looking at its suppliers and a supplier looking at its customers. The focus should be on communicating clearly and adopting a continuous improvement process. It is also critical you understand that your individual objectives all converge into one: achieving Supply Chain Excellence.

19

Conclusion

"The horizon leans forward, offering you space to place new steps of change."

— Maya Angelou

Supply Chain Excellence is not a quick fix; it is a continuous process. Information technology is its enabler—but people are the key to leveraging technology, integrating systems and processes, and harnessing the energy of change to create the agility and synchronization needed to achieve Supply Chain Excellence. Because Supply Chain Excellence involves people and asks them to change their behavior and attitudes, achieving Supply Chain Excellence takes time. Think of GE, Dell, and Wal-Mart. Their supply chains' agility, synchronization, and excellence were not achieved overnight, but over a number of years and after both failed initiatives and successful improvements.

Achieving Supply Chain Excellence also takes patience and perseverance—and a Revolution. You and your organization can create this Revolution. The tools are there, and they are not difficult to master. The main things to keep in mind are:

- Supply Chain Excellence is beyond SCM.
- You must move through six levels in sequence to achieve Supply Chain Excellence.
- Supply Chain agility is achieved when you harness the energy of change.
- Know your customers and plan for their needs and expectations.
- Supply Chain Excellence demands the synchronization of supply with demand throughout the supply chain.
- Supply Chain Excellence will result in awesome organizational success.
- Supply Chain Excellence is a supply chain's path forward.
- "When you come to a fork in the road, take it!" — Yogi Berra.

A supply chain can truly achieve Supply Chain Excellence, and you can ensure that there are No Boundaries in your supply chain. Choose a direction and begin the journey. Think of the people you'll meet on the way and consider how you can persuade them to join you on this journey. And, as Mr. Berra advises, take that fork in the road. You'll be glad you did and so will they.

GO! GO! GO!

Works Consulted

Books and Reports

Bennis, W. *On Becoming a Leader.* Phoenix:: Perseus, 1994.

Dell, Michael and Catherine Fredman. *Direct from Dell: Strategies That Revolutionized an Industry.* New York:: HarperBusiness, 1999.

Davis, Stanley M. *Blur: The Speed of Change in the Connected Economy.* Reading, MA: Addison-Wesley, 1998.

Jacobs, Stephen E., Michael D. Michaux, and Nilhan M. Ulusoy. *Industrial Growth: Industrial Distribution Overview.* U.S. Bancorp Piper Jaffray, 2001

Tompkins, James A. and Dale Harmelink, eds. *The Distribution Management Handbook.* Boston, MA.: McGraw Hill, 1994.

Tompkins, James A. and Jerry D. Smith, eds. *The Warehouse Management Handbook..* Raleigh, NC: Tompkins Press, 1998.

Tompkins, James A. *Winning Manufacturing: The How-To Book of Successful Manufacturing.* Norcross, GA: Industrial Engineering and Management Press, 1989.

Tompkins, James A., *Future Capable Company: What Manufacturing Leaders Need to Do Today to Succeed Tomorrow.* Raleigh, NC: Tompkins Press, 2001.

Tompkins, Jim. *Revolution: Take-Charge Strategies for Business Success.* Raleigh, NC: Tompkins Press, 1998.

Monographs

Tompkins Associates, Inc. *Achieving Logistics Excellence Through Supply Chain Synthesis.* Raleigh, NC: Tompkins Press, 1999.

_____. *Crossdocking in the Future.* Raleigh, NC: Tompkins Press, 1998.

_____. *Designing a Distribution Network to Address Today's Challenges.* Raleigh, NC: Tompkins Press, 1998.

_____. *Inventory: the Unwanted Asset.* Raleigh, NC: Tompkins Press, 1997.

_____. *The Journey to Warehousing Excellence.* Raleigh, NC: Tompkins Press, Tompkins Press, 1999.

_____. *Warehouse Management Systems Technologies.* Raleigh, NC: Tompkins Press, 1998.

Articles

"A Master Class in Radical Change," *Fortune* (13 December 1993).

"Built-to-Order as New Business Strategy," *New Straits Times* (3 April 2002.)

"E-Commerce Update." *Distribution Channels* (June 1999).

"Overheard." *Selling Power* (October 1999).

"Quote of the Week." *Information Week* (18 October 1999).

"Re-engineering the Supply Chain: One Company's Strategy." *Industry Week Solutions Guide* (October 1999).

"Software Tools: The Quick and the Dead." *Modern Materials Handling* (October 1999).

"Survey: Top Performers Cut SCM Costs to 4 Percent of Sales." *Modern Distribution Management* (21 October 1999).

"Up Front." *Logistics* (February 1998).

"UPS Group to Help Ford Streamline New Car Delivery." *Raleigh News and Observer,* (3 February 2000).

Allnoch, Allen, "Efficient Supply Chain Practices Mean Big Savings to Leading Manufacturers." *IIE Solutions* (July 1997).

Anderson, David L., Frank F. Britt, and Donavon J. Favre, "The Seven Principles of Supply Chain Management." *Supply Chain Management Review* (Spring 1997).

Baer, Tony, "E-business Transforms Manufacturing." *Manufacturing Systems* (July 1999).

Boyle, Matthew, "The Shiniest Reputations in Tarnished Times," *Fortune* (4 March 2002)

Bylinsky, Gene, "For Sale: Japanese Plants in the U.S." *Fortune* (February 2000).

Bradley, Peter, "Logistics Product." *Logistics* (July 1998).

Brooks, Rick, "Alienating Customers Isn't Always a Bad Idea, Many Firms Discover." *New York Times* (7 January 1999).

Brown, Stuart F., "Wresting New Wealth from the Supply Chain." *Fortune* (9 November 1998).

Cook, James Aaron, "Tool Time." *Logistics Tech* (March 1999).

Copacino, William C. and Jonathan L.S. Byrnes, "How to Become a Supply Chain Master," *Supply Chain Management Review* (September /October 2001.)

Coronna, Mark, "E-Commerce to E-Business." *Inbound Logistics* (September 1999).

Fine, Charles H., "The Ultimate Core Competency." *Fortune* (29 March 1999).

Gentry, Connie, "The Price of Progress: Affordable E-Commerce." *Inbound Logistics* (November 1998).

Gilmore, Dan, and James A. Tompkins, "Get Me a Real WMS." *IDS* (March 1999).

Gilmore, Dan, and James A. Tompkins, "The Value of Logistics Is on the Rise." *IDS* (November 1999).

Godin, Patty, "A New Scheduling Regime." *IIE Solutions* (June 1999).

Godin, Patty, "Growing a Global Economy." *Competitive Edge* (Winter 1999).

Gould, Janet, "Technology Focus." *IDS* (June 1999).

Gould, Janet, "The Internet Turns the Manufacturing Paradigm Upside Down." *IDS* (June 1999).

Grackin, Ann, "Opportunities Flourish in the e-World." *Competitive Edge* (Winter 1999).

Handfield, Robert B., and Daniel R. Krause, "Think Globally, Source Locally." *Supply Chain Management Review* (Winter 1999).

Hewitt, Fred, "Global Pipeline Management: Beyond SCM." *Supply Chain Management Review* (Winter 1999).

Hoffman, Kurt C., "The Vision: Suppliers, Manufacturers, Retailers Collaborating as One." *Global Sites and Logistics* (June 1998).

Kahl, Steven J., "What's the Value of Supply Chain Software?" *Supply Chain Management Review* (Winter 1999).

Kilbane, Doris, "The Secrets to EDI's Staying Power." *Automatic ID News* (October 1999).

Kirsner, Scott, "The Customer Experience." *Net Company* (Fall 1999).

Knill, Bernie, "IT Strikes Back: The Sequel." *Material Handling Engineering* (October 1998).

Krass, Louis John, "Building a Business Case for Supply Chain Technology." *Supply Chain Management Review* (Winter 1999).

LaLonde, Bernard J., "The Quest for Supply Chain Integration." *Supply Chain Management Review* (Winter 1999).

Landry, John T., "Supply Chain Management: The Case for Alliances." *Harvard Business Review* (November/December 1998).

Laseter, Timothy M., "Integrating the Supply Web." *Supply Chain Management Review* (Winter 1999).

Leon, Mark, "Brushing Up on Supply Chain." *Consulting Magazine* (November 1999).

Magretta, Joan, "The Power of Virtual Integration: An Interview with Dell Computer's Michael Dell." *Harvard Business Review* (March/April 1998).

Malone, Robert, "An Alliance for Progress." *Inbound Logistics* (June 1999).

Marien, Edward J., "Demand Planning and Sales Forecasting: A Supply Chain Essential." *Supply Chain Management Review* (Winter 1999).

McManus, John, "A Weather Watch." *American Demographics* (October 1999).

Olsen, Robert L., "Building a Better Supply Chain." *Competitive Edge* (Spring 1999).

Olsen, Robert L., "The Internet May Not Be the End of the Road for EDI." *Frozen Food Age* (October, 1999)

Parker, Kevin, "New Fundamentals." *Manufacturing Systems* (July 1999).

Pascale, Richard, Mark Millemann, and Linda Gioja, "Changing the Way We Change." *Harvard Business Review* (November/December 1997).

Pavis, Theta, "Digging for Data and Dollars." *Warehousing Management* (November/December 1999).

Purkiss, Mark, "Paperless is More: Warehousing Today and into the 21st Century." *Automatic ID News Europe* (September 1999).

Quinn, Franis J., "The Payoff!" *Logistics Management* (December 1997).

Reeve, James M., "The Financial Advantages of the Lean Supply Chain." *Supply Chain Management Review* (March/April 2002.)

Robertson, Robert, "Take That One: Pick-to-Light Systems Made Easy." *Materials Management and Distribution* (August 1999).

Salcedo, Simon, and Ann Grackin, "The e-Value Chain." *Supply Chain Management Review* (Winter 2000).

Schlegel, Gregory L., "Supply Chain Optimization: A Practitioner's Perspective." *Supply Chain Management Review* (Winter 1999).

Sparks, Debra, "Special Report: Partners." *Business Week* (25 October 1999).

Stein, Tom , "Agile Anywhere Takes Supply chains Online." *Information Week* (21 June 1999).

Swanton, Bill, "Managing the Change That E-Business Brings." *Software Strategies* (November/Decmeber 1999).

Tompkins, James A., "Demand Flow Leadership." *EC World* (February 1997).

_____. "Earnings Across the Supply Chain." *Supply Chain Technology New* (September/October 1999).

_____. "Enhancing the Warehouse's Role through Customization." *Warehousing Education and Research Council Special Report* (February 1997).

_____. "Who's Walking Who?" *Automatic ID News Europe* (October 1999).

_____. "Supply Chain Flow: James Tompkins on Supply Chain Synthesis." *Supply Chain Flow* (August 1998).

Tompkins, James A., Bernie Knill, and Tom Andel, "Time to Rise Above Supply Chain Management." *Supply Chain Flow* (Supplement, October 1998).

Tompkins, Jim and Forsyth Alexander, "e- Comes of Age." *Competitive Edge* (Winter 1999).

Trommer, Diane, "As 'Build to Order' Fires Up the PC Business, Can the Supply Chain Stand the Heat?" *Electronic Buyer's News* (15 December 1997).

Vasilash, Gary S., "The Real World." *Automotive Manufacturing and Production* (July 1998).

Weil, Marty, "Some Assembly Required." *Manufacturing Systems* (August 1999).

White, Gregory L., "How GM, Ford Think Web Can Make Splash on the Factory Floor." *Wall Street Journal* (9 November 1999).

Web Sites and Web Articles

"3PLs on the Rise: Outsourcing Is In!" *Modern Materials Handling,* http://www.manufacturing.net/pur/ (December 2001)

"AK Steel's Rockport Works Wins Prestigious Maintenance Honor; Becomes Second AK Steel Plant to Achieve Award," http://www.aksteel.com (4 February 2002)

"Business' Killer App: The Web," http://www.businessweek.com (15 April 2002)

"Customer Case Study: Roche Labs," http://www.stelingcommerce.com

"DCs Weigh the Value of Supply Chain Efficiencies," http://www.manufacturing.net (1 April 2002.)

"Exel Develops European Hub for International Rectifier," http://www.exel.com

"External Collaboration-Sears and Michelin," http://www.retailsystems.com (16 June 2002)

"John Deere Commercial Products - Winning at the Racetrack," http://www.manufacturing.net (1 April 2002)

"Johnson Varies Business Game," http://news.yahoo.com (1 June 2002)

"Juniper Networks Success Story," http://www.valdero.com (2002)

"Lean Operations: Plant Cuts Leaders, Empowers Workers," http://www.freep.com (14 June 2002)

"Logility Announces i-Commerce Strategy," http://www.logility.com (27 July 1999).

"Malcolm Baldrige National Quality Award: 2001 Award Recipient, Manufacturing Category," http://www.nist.gov (12 March 2002)

"Michael Dell Has Some Advice for Old-Line Manufacturers: Change Your Business Model," http://www.manufacturingnews.com (13 June 2000)

"Reebok Classic Presents a Blast from the Past," http://www.reebok.com (1 August 2002)

"Soligen Taps Kenmar Subsidiary Autotech to Market Its Rapid Metal Casting Technology for Automotive and Powertrain Applications," http://www.soligen.com (5 June 2001)

"Supply Chain Collaboration and Visibility," http://www.businessweek.com (August 2001)

"The Road from Craft Work to Agile Manufacturing." http://www.detroitnews.com (28 December 1999).

"Verizon Logistics - Making the Right Connections," http://www.manufacturing.net (1 April 2002)

Aiken, Joy, "Intel Corporation." http://www.hoovers.com (15 November 1999).

Associated Press, The, "Alliances Make Sense for Japanese Electronics Companies," http://news.yahoo.com (19 June 2002)

Barlas, Demir, "Honda's E-Business Strategy: Targeted spending in specific areas," http://line56.com (11 December 2001)

Bartlett's Quotes Online, http://www.bartleby.com.

Belkin, Gregory, "TrueValue Initiates CPFR with Delta Faucet," http://logistics.about.com (18 February 2002)

Carbo, Bob, "Align the Organization for Improved Supply Chain Performance," http://www.ascet.com (5 May 2002)

Carbone, James, "Design Moves into EMS Spotlight." http://www.manufacturing.net (17 January 2002.)

Carbone, James, "High-Tech Buyers See Tidal Wave of Opportunity." http://www.manufacturing.net (17 June 1999).

Carbone, Jim, "Contract Manufacturers Move to Vertical Integration," http://www.manufacturing.net (18 October 2001)

Carbone, Jim, "Good Riddance to 2001," http://www.manufacturing.net (20 January 2002)

Dicksteen, Lisa Napell, "Beauty Site Gets Personal with Oracle, WebSphere, E.piphany," http://techupdate.zdnet.com (1 October 2001)

Drickhamer, David, "Getting Down to Brass Tacks," http://www.iwvaluechain.com (4 December 2002)

Enck, David, and Forrest W. Breyfogle, "Six Sigma Goes Corporate," http://www.isixsigma.com (May 2002)

Frank's Creative Quotes from Famous People, http://www.bemorecreative.com.

Hannon, David, "Mavens More Cautious about B2B Expansion," http://www.manufacturing.net (18 July 2001)

Hill, Kimberly, "The Seven Deadly Sins of CRM," http://www.crmdaily.com (19 March 2002.)

Hirsh, Lou, "Whatever Happened to the E-Commerce Wow! Factor?" http://www.crmdaily.com (March 21, 2002.)

Krause, Joy, "Elevating the Recliner: Embattled Easy Chair Gains a Sense of Style," http://www.jsonline.com (26 May 2002)

Livingston, John , "Outsourcing IT," *Security Products,* http://www.secprodonline.com/ (January 2002)

Loudin, Amanda, "The Light Bulb Goes On," http://www.manufacturing.net (1 April 2002)

Loudin, Amanda, "Locking in Value," http://www.manufacturing.net (1 June 2002)

Maloney, David, "IKEA at Home on the Range," http://www.manufacturing.net/ (1 April 2002)

McPoland, Dennis, "Leading Trends That Will Impact the Food Supply Chain Over the Next Five Years," http://logistics.about.com (14 August 2001.)

Milligan, Brian. "Despite Attempts to Break Them, Functional Silos Live On." http://www.manufacturing.net/magazine/purchasing/ (4 November 1999).

Navas, Deb, "Collaborative Product Design," http://www.idsystems.com (May 2002)

Stedman, Craig, "Some Firms Use EDI Links to Trade Data, but Turn to Web for Real-time Planning," http://www.computerworld.com (15 November 1999).

Stundza, Tom, "Metals Service Centers—Looking for Answers," http://www.manufacturing.net (5 September 2001)

Vasilash, Gary S., "A Quick Look at Rapid Prototyping," http://www.autofieldguide.com (1 September 2001)

Vinas, Tonya, "Customer Order Management—Out of Order?" http://www.iwvaluechain.com (1 April 2002)

Voluntary Interindustry Commerce Standards (VICS) Association, The, "Collaborative Planning, Forecasting and Replenishment," http://www.cpfr.org (2001)

Index